Stepping Out Of ...

# You CAN beat depression,

# this is how

By Emma J Triplett

Stepping Out Of The Cloud

## Table of Contents

| | |
|---|---|
| INTRODUCTION | 4 |
| CHAPTER 1 – 'LIVING WITH DEPRESSION' | 10 |
| CHAPTER 2 – IT'S NOT YOUR FAULT | 18 |
| CHAPTER 3 – IS DEPRESSION AN ALLERGY? | 33 |
| CHAPTER 4 – BUT IT IS YOUR RESPONSIBILITY | 37 |
| CHAPTER 5 – FALSE BELIEFS ABOUT DEPRESSION | 50 |
| CHAPTER 6 – HOW DEPRESSION DEVELOPS | 64 |
| CHAPTER 7 – WHAT IS NEGATIVE THINKING? | 76 |
| CHAPTER 8 – THE STRESS BUCKET | 84 |
| CHAPTER 9 – WHY IS DEPRESSION EXHAUSTING? | 90 |
| CHAPTER 10 – THE BIOLOGICAL CAUSE | 95 |
| CHAPTER 11 – MAKING YOURSELF HAPPY | 99 |
| CHAPTER 12 – STEPPING OUT OF THE CLOUD | 101 |
| CHAPTER 13 – CHEMICAL BALANCE | 102 |
| CHAPTER 14 – WHAT YOUR DOCTOR | 112 |
| DOESN'T TELL YOU ABOUT ANTIDEPRESSANTS | 112 |
| CHAPTER 15 – CHEMICAL CONSUMPTION | 116 |
| CHAPTER 16 - CAUGHT IN THE DOWNPOUR | 119 |
| CHAPTER 17 – HOW TO REBALANCE YOUR CHEMICALS | 121 |
| CHAPTER 18 – WHY PRACTICE? | 132 |
| CHAPTER 19 – STEP BY STEP | 136 |
| CHAPTER 20 – HOW TO PRACTICE POSITIVE THINKING | 140 |
| CHAPTER 21 – RELAPSE RATE | 152 |
| CHAPTER 22 – LIVING ON CLOUD 9 | 157 |

| | |
|---|---|
| CHAPTER 23 – THE SECRET | 160 |
| CHAPTER 24 - MINDFULNESS | 165 |
| CHAPTER 25 – CHANGE | 171 |
| CHAPTER 26 – LIFE BALANCE | 176 |
| CHAPTER 27 – BASIC HUMAN NEEDS | 183 |
| CHAPTER 28 – SOCIAL LIFE AND INTERESTS | 187 |
| CHAPTER 29 – SUBCONSCIOUS WIRING | 195 |
| CHAPTER 30 – CREATING REALITY FROM IMAGINATION | 204 |
| CHAPTER 31 – YOUR SUBCONSCIOUS SUPERPOWERS | 209 |
| CHAPTER 32 – SUMMARY | 220 |
| CHAPTER 33 – THE FINAL WORD | 224 |
| ADDENDUM 1 – SELF HYPNOSIS MP3 | 227 |
| ADDENDUM 2 – MINDFULNESS MEDITATION PRACTICE | 228 |
| FURTHER READING | 229 |
| ABOUT THE AUTHOR | 230 |
| CONTACT INFORMATION | 231 |
| LEGAL NOTICES | 232 |
| DEDICATIONS | 233 |

# **Introduction**

Getting stuck in a big black cloud of despair and hopelessness where you feel isolated and lonely can seem eternal if not terminal. You have no energy and you've lost interest in everything, even life itself sometimes. You want to find a cure and you've tried everything but nothing works. You just can't find the way out.

As a therapist, and as someone who has had a brush with depression, I understand how hard having depression is when you are depressed.

Other people tell you to 'cheer up' or 'snap out of it' – helpful huh? That's like saying to someone with anxiety 'don't worry'. They clearly have no idea what it's like, if you could just snap out of it, you would have done so instantly, would you not? After all it's no fun having depression, no one would choose it, right?

The truth is, you are inadvertently doing just that – but that's not your fault, you're not doing it on purpose and your not doing it knowingly. The problem is you've been conditioned from an early age to be depressed and no one has every taught you how not to be.

All that changes now if you choose.

If you want to learn how to be 'undepressed' aka 'happy' 24/7 (yes even learning how to have happy healthy beneficial sleep) I am going to teach you step by step.

Is it going to be easy? – Not always,

But this is the easiest and quickest path to happiness, contentment, excitement and joy or whatever personal journey or goal you have in mind.

Can you do it? – Yes, without a doubt.

I say that with such confidence for two reasons:-

I have helped literally hundreds of people beat depression, it is a simple easy to learn step by step process everyone can do when they have decide they want to.

The fact that you are reading this tells me that you are ready to take action and do something for yourself, you are looking for answers, you've just found them.

You made the decision to take that step and buy this book, if you can do that, you can do this and I will be there to support and help you. Don't forget you can reach out to me by email any time you need some extra support.

You can do it, the only thing that will hold you back is your own belief and self talk that you can't. So I want you to drop that right now and start believing in yourself – I believe in you.

Climbing out of depression is just like any journey:

Initially, like today perhaps, you are full of anticipation and enthusiasm, it's the start of something new and exciting, you've packed your bags and you're off.

However, the middle bit of the journey can get a bit boring and tedious. If it's a long journey inevitably there will be delays along the way, things don't always run smoothly and there will be occasions when you will be fed up and wish you hadn't started and maybe you will think of turning back.

Don't turn back. Instead imagine the excitement of arriving; think of those times when you've gone on holiday - you arrive, exhausted but happy that you have finally got there and you can start the fun.

This is going to be exactly like that. The hardest part will be the middle when you might have a bad day and you're struggling to motivate yourself. If this doesn't happen, then you're not normal, remember that.

The difference between someone who overcomes their depression and someone who gives up and returns to their former unhappy black hole comfort zone is that resolve to dig deeper and find that inner resolve to put one foot in front of the other and keep going.

You will take the journey at your own pace, there is no one telling you how fast or slowly you 'should' come out of depression, it all depends on you. So the next mental shift I want you to make is to drop any comparison, preconceived ideas or judgment you might have of what should happen and how quickly. There is no benchmark, there is just you.

It will get easier and easier as you practice, but it is a practice.

For those of us who are no longer depressed, it is something we continue to practice every day, sometimes consciously, sometimes unconsciously, but being happy is a daily practice for anyone and everyone and some people do it unconsciously most of the time.

During the course of this book I will explain why that is and how to do it. At times I will tell you things you don't want to hear or things that conflict with your own beliefs, remember I have no interest in telling you anything but the truth and I'm telling you things you need to hear and understand for you to come out of depression and stay out permanently.

Take a moment to read the next few lines, then, close your eyes, take a nice deep breath and look into the future; imagine yourself with a big smile on your face, you're happy again.

Where are you?

What are you doing?

Is anyone with you?

Take in all the sight, smells and sounds around you, allow those feelings of peace, calm and joy to come through, they are there within you, deep inside and you can access them right now if you choose.

Take a few moments to relax and fully breath into the happy image, then open your eyes

## Are You Ready?

Before we start, I would like to draw your attention to Addendum 1 on page 230 - I have included a website address where you can download a free Self Hypnosis MP3 that you can listen to alongside this book with full instructions of how best to use it.

# Part 1

## Getting Depressed

## The truth about Depression

## - Why You?

# Chapter 1 – 'Living with Depression'

Who says you have to live with it?

'Living with depression' is a phrase invented by depressed people who don't understand how to cure themselves of depression.

In itself this is a potentially damaging phrase as it appeals to the negative 'hopeless' mindset of depression.

"There's no point trying, can't do anything about it, I will just have to learn to live with it".

The characteristics of 'depression thinking' are negative, global, 'all or nothing' and 'it's all about me'. Plus symptoms of depression include difficulty in getting motivated and feelings of despair and hopelessness, so the phrase 'living with depression' will resonate with someone who is depressed and give them an opt out for taking responsibility for doing anything about it.

The internal dialogue will go along the lines of

"I will NEVER be cured of depression, it's something I'm going to have to live with and there is NOTHING I can do about it so there's no point trying, I will ALWAYS have depression"

or "It's part of who I am, it's part of my personality".

Every one of these self sabotaging statements is NOT true, but the danger occurs because that person who now believes there is no choice in the situation will not try to do anything, give up and resign themselves that it's something they will have to live with for the rest of their life.

Don't invite depression into your house, to live with you and don't accept it as part of who you are. Depression is a temporary illness, treat it as such.

## Where is your evidence coming from?

Neurologically, your brain will look for evidence to back a statement up that you believe or want to be true – and it will find it. Your brain will find whatever it's looking for.

You get on the Internet and you find people on social media describing themselves in their profile as 'living with depression' - **evidence?**

You try some of the remedies you discover for a week or two – nothing happens instantly - **evidence?**

You talk to lots of people about it, describing how bad you feel, all your symptoms, how bad life is and, in their well-intentioned but ill-informed attempt to make you feel better, they tell you about all the other people they know who have had depression for years - **evidence?**

You find people who have had depression for 20 years and are 'experts' on the condition who tell you it's something you have to live with - **evidence?**

People tell you their depression is hereditary and you realise your mum has depression – **evidence that it's out of your control?**

You go to the doctor and get diagnosed with 'clinical depression' - it sounds wonderfully serious, doesn't it. But be careful of 'labels', they are disempowering. So you are labeled 'clinically depressed' or something equally traumatic – **evidence?**

The doom and gloom deepens, the black cloud gets thicker and your belief that there's nothing you can do is reinforced, so you resign yourself to 'this is something I'm going to have to 'cope with' for the rest of my life.

# Rubbish!

Let's destroy the myth that you have to 'live with depression' once and for all…

First of all, let's take a closer look at the so called 'evidence' above :-

They are **opinions** of people who are depressed who are justifying their depression. It is more comfortable to find something to blame than it is to face up to the responsibility of doing something about it.

It didn't take you two weeks to get depressed, it's going to take a little bit longer than that to get better, but one of the symptoms of depression is lack of motivation, so sticking at anything with conviction and belief is not second nature right now, but it can be.

Depression is one of the most common conditions in the modern world – 1 in 4 people a year in the UK alone experience symptoms of anxiety and/or depression, anyone you talk to will know someone who has it – that does not mean it's for life or there is nothing YOU can do.

'Clinical depression' just means you have at least 5 of the recognised symptoms for two weeks or more, it doesn't mean permanent or terminal.

There is no scientific evidence that it is hereditary (passed on in genes), but there is evidence that, if there is family history of depression, you are 8 times more likely to develop it – these two things are NOT the same. But people hear 'family history' and wrongly assume that means 'hereditary' or it's in the genes.

You were not born depressed, you learn how to be depressed as you grow up. If there is depression or anxiety in the household you grew up in, your thought patterns and behaviour will have been influenced negatively and you will think and behave in a similar way. We have a group of brain cells called 'mirror neurons' which helps us learn by mimicking those around it, but they don't discriminate between learning good and bad things, they just mimic.

People who have had depression for a long time, or several bouts of it, are NOT experts on depression, they may be experts on how to stay depressed or how to have depression again and again, but they are NOT experts on how to cure depression so don't listen to them. It is comfortable for them to draw people into their tribe of 'living with depression', one because we are tribal and want to fit in, but also it means they're not a lone failure, they can find other people who are struggling, therefore it's not their responsibility to do anything different.

I had a comment last week on a Facebook post I had promoted, from a guy objecting to me posting a free video called 'How depression develops'. Without even watching it (I know he didn't because he didn't sign up to get the video) he declared it as 'rubbish' (typical negative thinking of a depressed person). Someone else then posted, 'you sound as if you know a lot about depression'. His reply was "yes I do, I've had depression for years and I know lots of other people with it". This makes him good at having depression, it doesn't mean he knows a lot about depression and he clearly doesn't know how to cure himself.

Sadly ignorance and arrogance is the formula for staying depressed, not the cure. He was completely unwilling to open his mind to watching something that would have helped, sadly I suspect he will stay depressed for along time.

The good news is that depression it's not permanent, you just need to learn how to change it and this book will teach you how to do that.

Dropping the ego and learning new things is empowering. If you can open your mind to new concepts and ideas, you can be cured.

## Evidence that you DON'T have to LIVE WITH depression from credible medical sources

The following quotes are from clinical and medical websites – the links are provided if you want to check it out for yourself

NHS UK

"The good news is that with the right treatment and support, most people can make a full recovery."

## American Psychiatric Association

"Depression is among the most treatable of mental disorders. Between 80 percent and 90 percent of people with depression eventually respond well to treatment. Almost all patients gain some relief from their symptoms."

## Rethink Mental Illness

Depression is:

- a mental illness that is recognised worldwide.
- common. It affects about one in ten of us.
- something that anyone can get.
- treatable.

Depression is not:

- something you can 'snap out of.'
- a sign of weakness.
- something that everyone experiences.
- something that lasts forever.

## Royal College of Psychiatrists

- Many other people have had depression.
- It may be hard to believe, but you will eventually come out of it.
- Depression can sometimes be helpful – you may come out of it stronger and better able to cope. It can help you to see situations and relationships more clearly.

- You may be able to make important decisions and changes in your life, which you have avoided in the past.

## NIMH (National Institute of Mental Health)

Depression, even the most severe cases, can be treated. The earlier that treatment can begin, the more effective it is.

I particularly want to draw your attention to the statement from WebMD

## WebMD

…. people with depression sometimes fail to realise (**or accept**) that **there is a biological cause** to their depressed moods. As a result, they may **search endlessly for external causes.**

So with this 'medical evidence' why do you notice the bad 'evidence' that tells you that you have to live with it and not the actual medical facts?

There are two reasons

1. Because someone with depression will think in terms of the worst possible scenario, and
2. You, or someone else you respect the opinion of, has labeled you as having depression which has given your subconscious brain an instruction to look out for and bring your attention to anything to do with depression, especially the negative stuff,

This is a natural primitive function of the brain that is part of our survival system. It kept us alive in primitive times, but it's no longer appropriate for modern lives, so it's not your fault your brain works in this way.

# Chapter 2 – It's Not Your Fault

## Paleo Mind vs Modern Man/Woman

As humans we are amazing, the complexity of the human body and mind and how it all intrinsically functions perfectly as one organism is wondrous; it is quite literally mind-boggling

We are perfectly designed –

## for living two hundred thousand years ago!

The modern world we live in today has changed beyond recognition from the world we were designed to thrive in, but our biological make-up hasn't changed and this is at the root of what is going wrong and central to putting it right.

Our brains have developed an incredible intellect that drives change and advances in our evolution and society, but the original operating system in our brains cannot be updated. New programmes can be added and we've managed to adapt, but as life speeds up and technological advances introduce new circumstances and conditions, our brain doesn't have a template for optimum operating; all it can do is apply the original programme and unfortunately that doesn't always fit automatically, sometimes it needs manual input.

Modern life has got carried away with technology and progress, not necessarily a bad thing, but we need to learn to live our modern lives within our original operating system and thrive, not fall apart at the seams and then be patched up and held together with medication because our basic needs are not addressed.

## A short lesson in evolution

We have been evolving at an incredible rate in the last few hundred years. To put this in perspective, if you were to reframe the period from the first modern humans two hundred thousand years ago to today into the space of a calendar year, it would look something like this:

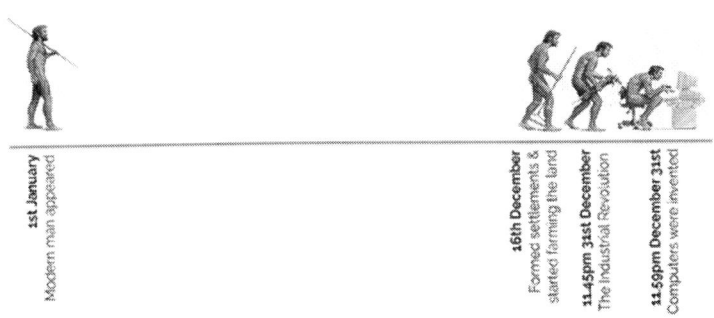

- On 1st January, modern man first appeared
- On 16th December, human started to form settlements and farm the land
- At 11.45pm on December 31st, the Industrial Revolution happened (machines were invented)
- At 11.59pm on December 31st, Computers were invented.

If you had a time machine and went back two hundred thousand years and brought Paleo man back with you into our modern day world, would you expect him (or her) to adapt and thrive? You probably wouldn't expect him to even stay alive for very long, at the very best he would go a little bit crazy, but that is exactly what our brains have had to do and it's evidence of how incredible we are that we have survived. However, as our modern lives and technology are still progressing at a rapidly increasing pace, the gap between our blueprint and our modern life is increasing to the point where we are breaking down.

Our brain is not a computer, so unfortunately we can't plug something in which updates the original operating system.

As we have evolved, we have developed an immense intellect, something other animals haven't managed as well as humans, which is why you don't generally see dogs driving around in cars or chatting to each other on mobile phones. Our human intellect is incredible, it is the reason for our rapid evolution, why we are the dominant species on the planet, why we can now take to the air, land on the moon and invent and understand things way beyond the comprehension of the geniuses of the day just two hundred years ago.

But, in the same instance, it is beginning to backfire and we are breaking, mentally and physically.

We have physical conditions linked to our nervous system that just did not exist even a short while ago – ME, MS, Fibromyalgia, IBS, eczema and asthma are all affected, if not yet proven to be caused, by our nervous system.

Emotional and mental health problems, so rapidly on the increase today, such as depression and anxiety, OCD, eating disorders, self harm and bipolar, did not exist very long ago. According to the World Health Organisation, by the year 2020 depression will be the leading cause of disease in the world.

And there's more, we actually had this vast intellectual resource all those years ago, but because life wasn't as complex then, we were more attuned to listening to it, we were more in touch with the operating instructions, there wasn't so much white noise and information cluttering up the channels, it was simpler and we were more able to use it effectively.

Our cleverness has forgotten our origins, but understanding the important elements of our blueprint, where this has gone wrong and what we need to do to emulate that blueprint gives us all the tools we need to live happy, mentally and physically healthy lives and take full advantage of the opportunities and tools available to us in this modern world.

## Why Modern Life Doesn't Fit with Slowly Evolving Humans

Well, to put it simply there is a huge disparity between how we were designed and how we live today.

There are three fundamental areas that have gone wrong, but we don't need to use our imaginations too much to see how things should work.

Have you ever travelled to a Third World or 'Developing' country?

What's the first thing you notice about the people there?

## They are happy.

Despite the poverty, despite not having enough food to eat, despite not having TV, mobile phones, computers, the latest trainers, cars, holidays and the internet so they can order an abundance of goodies to be delivered to their door – they are happy.

This is in contrast to the so called 'Developed' world where all these things are available, but one in ten adults suffers from depression at some time during their life.

How could it be that the 'developing world' has happiness whilst the 'developed world' has depression – that doesn't make sense does it?

Well, yes it does actually, if you look at our blueprint.

People in 'developing' countries are living a lifestyle much closer to that of our primitive ancestors:

| Developing World Lifestyle | Western World Lifestyle |
| --- | --- |
| People live in large extended family and tribal units. They support each other, they learn from people they respect and trust and how to live is passed down through generations. They share | People live in small isolated groups. It's not unusual for people to live alone and isolated. Support and answers to problems are found on faceless, soulless computers. |

You can beat depression, this is how.

| | |
|---|---|
| tasks, they support each other, when things are tough, they come together and help each other.<br><br>Everyone has a defined role within the family or community, elders have a respected role, the burden of survival is shared and everyone contributes.<br><br>Regular festivals and coming together of the community keeps face to face communication alive and if someone visits, they don't just visit for a couple of hours, they will often stay for days or weeks. | We don't need to interact with anyone, we can even get our food delivered to our door without seeing a soul.<br><br>Largely communication is through the means of technology, we text and email, we have very little face to face interaction.<br><br>Life is lived behind closed doors. Even just 100 years ago, it was much more community based with support coming from neighbours, but now it's easy to never even meet your neighbours. Visits are quick, we don't need to learn to get on with each other and our support is self obtained. |
| If someone needs to go somewhere, physical activity is inevitably involved. Many people are subsistence farmers which is hard labour | We get into a car or other transport, drive to our destination, get out and sit at a desk or something similar. We have spent much money |

| | |
|---|---|
| and without technology and electricity, many jobs and activities are labour intensive, but what they are getting from this is a sense of achievement. It may have taken two hours to prepare a meal, but the result is rewarding. | and many hours inventing labour saving devices which cost us money, so we have to work more hours in a sedentary job to buy these things because we're working too many hours to do the task without them. Where's the satisfaction in putting something in the microwave? |
| They can't afford to think negatively, they have to believe that every time they go out to work in the fields or go hunting, they are going to come home with food or the means to provide for themselves and their families. They cannot afford to think "there's no point planting the fields this year, last year there was a drought, it could happen again and they'll never grow", it's survival. Or if they're walking four hours to get water, they can't negatively forecast there | We have a social safety net and a society which not only allows, but encourages, negative thinking. The media bombards us constantly with negative stories of disaster, doom and gloom, complaints, injustice and dissatisfaction. We have a culture which promotes and encourages negativity in looking for something to complain about and it's rewarded with an audience. If we can't work for whatever reason, we have a government which will give us money, a house and food. |

| won't be water in the well and not bother. They have to think positively to get motivated in order to survive. | There is no necessity to be positive for our survival. |

We've moved so far away from our original design that we've lost the skills which help us survive and thrive - and I don't mean building shelters and hunting with spears and bows and arrows, I mean we don't behave in a natural way, we don't have the sense of achievement from hunting down a wild boar, preparing and cooking it, or living as part of a close community, they've been replaced by convenience and electronic entertainment and as a result, it's all going a bit wrong.

But it doesn't have to.

I'm not suggesting we all have to go back to basics, dig up the lawns and patios and plant our food, throw away the technology and live with our parents - Nooooo!

What I'm saying is that understanding the fundamental reasons and physiological effects behind our natural primitive behaviours allows us to innovate and replace those outdated forms of living which just don't fit in the modern world we've evolved, with other actions and activities which have the same effect on our body, mind and emotions and will keep us mentally healthy, functioning at our best in our new world.

## Why Modern Life Is Making Us Sick

## Technology

Although technology enhances our lives in many way, it has also taught us anxieties of a kind we wouldn't have had until recently.

## Speed of Communication.

We are very impatient these days and we can't deal with ambiguity, with not knowing. It was as recently as 25 years ago that most communication travelled by letter. People accepted having to wait; it was normal. Email has taken over from 'snail-mail' and so if we don't get answers by return, we start to wonder why and our imagination takes over. It's even more instant with text, if someone doesn't answer a text very quickly, we get frustrated and want to know why not, and because we don't know, we make it up in our heads or worry about not hearing back from that person. And what about apps like Whatsapp where we can even tell if someone has read our message or not - have you ever looked at that and got annoyed or impatient when you don't get a reply as quickly as you would like? In Facebook it shows you if someone is logged in and online, what goes around in your mind when someone doesn't reply to a message and you can see they are online?

## Computer Games

Computer games are designed to create anxiety. Our brain doesn't know the difference between imagination and reality, so when you're playing a computer game your brain thinks it's real and you will experience the feelings of anxiety, panic, elation etc just as if it was actually happening to you. It can also be addictive, just as survival is; when you do something right, you get rewarded with feeling pleased with yourself and your brain wants to do it again, but it's not real.

## Television

As with computer games, TV programmes, especially the news, soaps and drama series, suck us in to the anxiety and tension they create. They are also a form of distraction for our brains from the other stuff in our lives creating the anxiety and/or depression, but we are being distracted by one source of anxiety to another which is completely unnatural for us. We are also being bombarded with propaganda setting our expectation levels of how we should compare ourselves amongst our peers. Even if we consciously disagree or don't want that lifestyle, subconsciously, if we are not doing as well as the adverts on TV suggest, then we are not keeping up with evolution and therefore it creates anxiety.

## Too Clever

Having a big brain has its disadvantages, of course it has given us the ability to evolve as quickly as we have, especially in the last few hundred years, but the downside to having the vast intellect is that we overthink things.

People who suffer from anxiety and depression can be from all walks of life and it's certainly not something that just afflicts a certain demographic. But one of the common elements that all people with anxiety or depression are doing wrong is overthinking. In their attempts to figure out why they feel anxious or miserable, they analyse and imagine many different possible scenarios, going over and over things in their mind. This is not solving the problem, all it is actually doing is creating more anxiety and depression, keeping them locked in. They use their imagination to negatively forecast every possible future outcome, or try to imagine what other people are thinking or doing, without being aware that they are actually using their imagination to do this, instead they believe it as reality.

So being clever is a disadvantage if you're using your brain worrying about things that will never happen or re-examining everything you don't like about your life.

## Too Much Time

Having too much time to think is not good either. Nowadays we spend too much time on our own allowing our brains to negatively imagine and run through scenarios.

In primitive times, firstly people would not have been on their own just thinking very much at all, and secondly they didn't have time to think because they were too busy hunting and gathering and surviving.

In our progressive 'developed' world societies we have focused much time, effort and money inventing labour saving and time saving devices so we spend less time doing things that keep us mentally healthy and more time thinking about things we don't need to keep going over.

Some of the danger spots for too much thinking are:-

- The commute to work
- Driving
- Sitting in front of the TV
- Cleaning (with devices that don't need physical work)
- Any other time we are doing manual jobs on our own that don't require positive engagement of our brain.

When I lived in Nepal, I observed something interesting– people were hardly ever alone; even in tasks that only took one person, for example, cleaning the windows, there would always be at least two people doing it, and they never travelled alone. It's interesting that they are also the happiest people I've ever come across.

As people slide further into depression they do less and less, creating more and more thinking time. This thinking is negative, often introspecting about themselves and their lives; this is what causes the depression.

Before we had modern technology, cars, modern conveniences and labour saving devices, we wouldn't have had time to think. Our daily schedule would have been full of useful serotonin creating activities, we would have gone from one job to another and we would have interacted with people. If we had something on our mind the opportunity was always there to talk about it, but in today's society it is too easy to not talk about it at all, instead thinking about it too much and letting it grow out of normal perspective.

## Media Propaganda

In this age of information technology, information has become more accessible. In reality we have no idea how much of the information we're being fed is true but we can be sure of that most of it is negative.

Doom and gloom, crisis and disaster, terror and fear are newsworthy, you probably wouldn't be far wrong if you had the impression that all the news is negative these days, We are bombarded at every interval by the news on TV, newspapers and radio of criticism, negativity and disasters; at home or abroad it seems that news is not news unless it is there to scare us.

I remember in 2004, I was living in Kathmandu the capital of Nepal and at the time there was civil unrest; friction between the king, the government and the Maoist party, who wanted recognition and acceptance. As a foreigner living in Nepal the local politics didn't affect me, I wasn't a target. However, my family back in the UK knew every time there had been a bomb in the city or a problem as it was being reported on and sensationalised by the international press.

The journalists covering the stories sensationalise them with attention-grabbing headlines. We lose sight of the fact that the news is deliberately written to catch attention in order to sell their paper and not another one and the most effective thing to grab your attention is fear.

It is well known in the psychology of marketing that there are two elements you need to interrupt current thought and grab attention, and they are sex or fear. These are your baselines. If you want to promote anything you either need to show that somehow this product will make you more attractive to the opposite sex, or you promote the fear of not using the product.

There is a well-known clothes washing additive that you're encouraged to use on your wash in addition to your washing detergent because if you don't your clothes will come out stained and you will look dirty! Now when you think about it this is ridiculous, because why would you buy a detergent that doesn't clean properly on its own? You shouldn't need to buy another product to add to it to clean your clothes. But the advert suggests that if you don't you'll be judged as dirty.

Fear is promoted widely throughout our TV advertising - every which way we turn, we are bombarded with negativity in the media.

Our modern age of information technology is designed to create anxiety and keep the audience hooked in and we are unaware we're being manipulated in this way.

Advertisers, marketers and, indeed journalists are all tapping into the part of our brain that deals with fear. To human beings this is intoxicating because if your brain detects fear and anxiety it stays focused on the source. For people using psychology to sell us goods, ideas or news it's a very powerful tool. However, the side-effect is the subconscious effect it is having on a primitive part of our brain that becomes locked in survival mode, looking for more problems and possible dangers.

The result of this constant overstimulation of the fight/flight response is having a detrimental effect on our brains and we are not getting the chance to switch it off and allow our minds to settle.

The added overstimulation by the media, stress at work and modern expectations, combined with a reduction in activity and personal interaction, is leaving us unbalanced.

It is not your fault if you've ended up with anxiety and depression BUT it is your responsibility to fix it by learning how to adapt your life so you operate within your primitive blueprint whilst making the most of all the opportunities the modern world has to offer.

# Chapter 3 – Is Depression an Allergy?

There is recent research that is gaining ground scientifically that suggests depression is an allergic reaction.

When something 'foreign' enters the body, the immune system jumps into action. This is happening in the background all the time dealing with possible invaders without you knowing anything about it.

However, part of that immune system is inflammation set off by a family of proteins called cytokines and these also switch the brain into sickness mode.

Think of when you have a bad cold or flu – how do you feel? Tired, all you want to do is sleep, miserable, you lose interest in things, have difficulty in concentrating? Doesn't that sound a bit like depression?

Both cytokines and inflammation have been shown to rocket during depressive episodes and, in people with bipolar, they drop off during periods of remission.

The question scientists are now trying to answer is 'what sets off the inflammation?' We know infection does, but it is not the only trigger by any means, just as likely is allergies.

In Chapter 14, we look at how the consumption of chemicals affects our body and mind, the bombardment of artificial chemicals we ingest through the additives, colourings and preservatives in our foods and water are going to put pressure on the immune system.

When you get bitten or stung by an insect and their poison is injected into your body, your immune system reacts, sending white blood cells with antibodies to the area. For some people, their immune system reacts vigorously and swelling (inflammation) to a greater or lesser degree occurs in that area. Some people can have violent allergic reaction to specific poisons.

Things that we are not designed to cope with as part of our original blueprint could quite easily be causing the same allergic reaction and inflammation.

A diet rich in trans fats and sugar has been shown to promote inflammation, while a healthy one full of fruit, veg and oily fish helps keep it at bay. Obesity is another risk factor, probably because body fat, particularly around the belly, stores large quantities of cytokines.

Add this to the fact that stress, particularly the kind that follows social rejection or loneliness, also causes inflammation, and it starts to look as if depression is a kind of allergy to modern life.

Many foods we now eat on a daily basis in the Western world including grains such as wheat, pulses and sugars and some fats would not have been part of our primitive diet.

Perhaps this explains the spiraling prevalence of depression all over the world as we increasingly eat, sloth and isolates ourselves into a state of chronic inflammation.

The good news is that the few clinical trials done so far have found that adding anti-inflammatory medicines to antidepressants not only improves symptoms, it also increases the proportion of people who respond to treatment, although more trials will be needed to confirm this.

There is also some evidence that omega 3 and curcumin, an extract of the spice turmeric, might have similar effects. Both are available over the counter and might be worth a try, although as an add-on to any prescribed treatment – there's definitely not enough evidence to use them as a replacement.

The even better news is however that there are steps you can take immediately if inflammation is a contributory factor of your depression to work towards eliminating toxins from your diet and be mindful of what you are consuming.

There is no doubt whatsoever that when you eat a clean healthy diet, free from additives and preservatives, added salt and sugar you feel better. If chemical consumption and a consumption of certain 'foods' our bodies are not designed for is one cause of depression, which is looking more and more likely, what a lovely easy problem to be able to solve.

I would encourage you to look into the Paleo diet and lifestyle. Its theories are aligned with this book in that it promotes eating and exercising in a way that emulates our original primitive blueprint. Understanding the holistic approach to how we are designed, mind and body gives us the tools to correct the errors and distortions that have crept in over the last few centuries of the rapidly developing modern world.

I don't think it is any coincidence whatsoever that modern diseases such as depression seem to be increasing across the globe at an accelerating pace as 'modern life' and progress accelerates.

# Chapter 4 – But It Is Your Responsibility

That said and done, it's not your fault, but what do you do about it?

Lie down, roll over and accept it, take the pills and live in misery - or learn how to adapt and put your life right so you can be happy, motivated and energised.

And why is it that not everyone has depression?

What are you doing that people without depression are not, and vice versa?

If you want 'out' of depression, you can achieve it. No one has to live with depression, but if you've fallen into the depression trap as 1 in 10 people do, of waiting for someone to knock on your door with the magic pill to cure you, you are not going to get better in a hurry.

Take responsibility for learning a cure that is freely available for everyone, and you will get better.

Your first step is to accept it is your responsibility to look after your physical and mental health.

It doesn't help I know that we have developed a 'blame' culture where we're encouraged to find an external reason and therefore an external cure.

The cure is within you right now and we're going to help you find it and bring it to the surface so you will always be in control of your thoughts, feelings and actions.

## Current Medical Advice for curing depression

I really like the advice from the Royal College of Psychiatrists about depression and, having been there, I completely agree.

Royal College of Psychiatrists

Many other people have had depression.

It may be hard to believe, but you will eventually come out of it.

Depression can sometimes be helpful – you may come out of it stronger and better able to cope. It can help you to see situations and relationships more clearly.

You may be able to make important decisions and changes in your life, which you have avoided in the past.

'Depression can sometimes be helpful and you may be able to make important decisions and changes in your life which you have avoided in the past'

Without a doubt depression changed my life for the better and it may well be the best thing that every happened to me.

You see, I had become trapped in a lifestyle dictated by false belief, I was locked into believing that there was nothing else I could do to maintain my income level and I hated my job and career. When depression struck, it was my brain's way of telling me to stop. It had been telling me for a while, I knew I had to change but quite frankly it was easier to stay in the career and have the money than it was to get out, a case of 'better the devil I knew', so I dismissed my intuition that was screaming at me to live differently.

Not only that, my diet mainly consisted of convenience food, bread and pasta, that the things that I now know are not a natural part of our diet.

But, getting out was just too scary – 'what if I couldn't pay the mortgage and lost my house?' was my biggest fear.

In general the biggest fear of all human beings is ambiguity. We find it very difficult to deal with the unknown and what we can't control. Our imagination fills in the blanks and when we have anxiety or a lot of stress in our lives, those blanks are negative, we look at the worst possible scenario.

However, the depression forced me to stop, I shut down mentally and I eventually stopped thinking 'I can't', it swung towards 'I have to' before settling on 'How can I?'

I will tell you exactly what I did during the course of this book, but the point I want to make right now is that if I hadn't been forced into making significant changes in my life by the depression, I may well have just kept going around in the same unhappy circles and never found the path to the freedom I now have in my life and learned how to make myself happy.

I am most definitely stronger for having had depression and I now look at life from a different perspective.

My biggest fear when I was under that black cloud was that I would lose my house – it didn't happen, I didn't end up at poverty central, everything turned out fine and I literally am living happily ever after.

## An Uncommon Analogy for Depression

I want you to think about something else in your life that you have to manage or cope with on a daily basis – perhaps you have a physical disability or something else that affects your life.

For me weight management has many similarities to depression.

I am prone to putting on weight and if I were to eat what I wanted, when I wanted, I would be the size of a one bedroom detached bungalow! My 'hot spots' for eating are when I am bored or when I'm procrastinating.

I could blame it on genes, we're not a naturally skinny family!

I could also use the excuse that I have polycystic ovaries. If you haven't come across POS before, in a nutshell, I have insulin resistance which means if I eat sugars and simple carbohydrates, I over produce insulin which makes me crave sugars and simple carbohydrates. When I eat them, I am then extremely good at storing the excess sugars as fat. If I get on a binge, I will put on a stone a month until I stop. Depression is also a symptom of POS – coincidence – I don't think so!

I have reasons and excuses for being overweight and I also have choices.

I can choose to go with the reasons and excuses and get fat, hate myself and be miserable or I can manage it in my day to day life.

I know that when I am managing my weight properly I am fit, I feel fantastic, I'm confident and I'm happy. I'm more sociable and I enjoy life, the more I do, the more energy, enthusiasm and zest for life I have.

But when I'm not managing it well, I become lazy, I withdraw from everyone, I eat very badly and I put on more weight. I have no motivation or enthusiasm for anything, I'm miserable and I blame it on everything else, I stay in every evening, get bored and eat.

(Sounds a lot like depression, doesn't it?)

OK, so I have an extra factor in there that I have to manage, the POS that causes the binges, but I still have a choice and when I'm not eating sugars and simple carbohydrates, I'm not compelled to binge – simple, don't eat them (in theory!!)

There are times when I slip into bad habits and I start down the slippery slope and I put on weight, when I do It's a long haul back to healthy eating and fitness again.

I know it's worth it though, it might take three months to get back to my size 12, fit and happy again, but I get my determination on and I do it.

I could think of this in terms of 'living with being fat' – but I don't and for exactly the same reasons why I'm telling you to stop thinking in terms of 'living with depression'. It is a constant reminder of the worst bits and, as you will learn in later chapters, whatever you focus on will be invited into your life.

Starting now, I want you to think of it in terms of 'managing your happiness' in the same way I think of it in terms of managing my weight – or perhaps maintaining your happiness, as I maintain my weight.

Sometimes it is a struggle, sometimes I do slip, but the better I get at it, the longer the periods of wearing my lovely clothes become and I spend less time in my frumpy fat clothes.

To manage my weight or maintain my slim size there are things I have to do and things I can't do, whether I like it or not. So I remind myself how good I feel when I'm at my best and do it.

I've come to learn that it is no coincidence at all that modern life is having the same detrimental effect on people's weight as it is on their mental health.

Just as we have introduced conveniences and changed the social structure of modern lives that conflicts with our primitive blueprint, our diets have become distorted and changed, also in relatively recent modern times.

It is only about ten thousand years ago that we started settling down, forming communities and farming, introducing grains, pulses and legumes into our diets. These would not have been a large part of our diet as they are today. Also in nature you do not find the fat + sugar combination that is so prevalent in our modern diets; cakes, biscuits and even bread are a modern invention. Our bodies are amazing at adapting and coping with what we choose to consume, but if like me, you have a system that doesn't cope so well but you want to stay fit and healthy you have to be vigilant about what you consume and make choices.

I have spent most of my life a vegetarian (from the age of 15), but as I've got older I have had to make a choice

Either:-

Eat meat again or be fat

I'm not saying that is the same for everyone, I have learned through trial, error and managing my weight that the things I used to eat a lot of; pasta, lentils, wheat, grains, etc are the things that promote my weight gain whereas if I stick to a high protein, low carb diet, my weight doesn't fluctuate.

So, for the greater good (in my case feeling fantastic, confident and happy), I have to make sacrifices, not do things I would like to do and I have to do some things I would prefer not to do.

It wasn't easy learning to eat meat again, it's taken a massive shift in mindset and it didn't happen overnight, but it was a choice.

The reason I'm telling you this as a very closely related analogy is because it is going to take the same principals for you to get out of depression:-

## A mindset shift.

You are going to need to open your mind to new concepts and ways of thinking and living that could well contradict many things that you have believed for a long time – certainly throughout your liaison with depression. If you have it now, something about what you believe or the way you think has to change.

## I wasn't born fat – You weren't born depressed.

But along the way, we did some bad learning and/or something has gone wrong with our physiological makeup and we now have to make changes to our beliefs and lifestyle and relearn a better way.

## Modern life has got in the way.

It is certainly true that so called 'progress' has distorted the naturally healthy physical and mental balance of humans. We can't go back, but we can adapt and it's up to us to do it.

## Medication

If there was a pill I could take that would keep me a healthy UK size 10 or 12, I probably would, it would be a lot easier, but there isn't. There are things you can take to help you lose weight, but they are not intended for long term use or for weight maintenance.

There is no difference at all with anti-depressants. They are not going to make you happy, but they help to get you to the start line. You cannot take them in order to maintain your happiness, you need to learn how to do that yourself.

Taking antidepressants alone is like taking a pill in the morning to stop you absorbing the fat and sugar then stuffing cake in your mouth all day.

The problem with depression is that no one teaches you what to do instead of the 'eating cake' bit. You keep doing the same things; you will keep getting the same results.

This book is going to teach you what you are doing that is making you depressed and what you can do instead to make you happy.

# Exercise 1 – Your Depression Diet

As with any diet, it's not just a case of cutting out what is unhealthy for you, if you want long term success and not the yoyo diet or mental health yoyo, you need to adapt your lifestyle. Exercise 1 helps you to understand what is unhealthy for your mind and make necessary adjustments.

As with a healthy lifestyle, it's not always necessary to adopt an all or nothing approach. You don't need to make yourself miserable by saying you can never eat a biscuit again, you can have one or two, just don't eat the whole packet and this is what I'm suggesting with the following 'depression diet'.

## The Media

The media is not just a source of depression; it is also a source of anxiety. Anxiety and depression often coexist, we are very good at switching between the two, therefore, exercise 1 is about imposing a media blackout in your life.

1. **Complete Blackout on the news – TV, radio and newspapers**

    You will not miss out on what is going on in the world, you will still get to hear about events, but from active listening and conversation, not the damaging subliminal anxiety inducing subconscious programming that comes from taking in the sensationalised headlines and juicy bits the media throws out to grab attention.

Trust me on this one, I have not listened to the news on TV or bought a newspaper for years and I'm still up with current affairs. The news will still leak into your life and if you want to find out more about something, you can intentionally go online and find out.

**2. Watch TV with intention, not by default**

Surprised you there didn't I? Perhaps you thought I was going to say no TV. Goodness, no! I would be a complete hypocrite if I said that, I couldn't live without Netflix box sets!!

What I mean here is set yourself a time or limit and watch programmes you are interested in. Do not switch on the TV as soon as you get home and have it droning in the background. For example, set an intention to switch the TV on only after 8pm or until 10pm. Most programmes you can watch on replay these days, but if you can't miss Eastenders at 7.30pm on a Tuesday and Thursday, watch it, then switch off the TV off half an hour earlier than you normally would.

In the times when there is no TV, find something else to do, listen to an audiobook, put music on and do something else, even if it is something small. You will be amazed at how many hours you gain in your life when you switch the TV off.

**3. Don't live by Social Media – take advantage of it.**

It is easy to stay in contact with nearest and dearest by social media programs and convenience 'aps' on your phone. Text messaging in one form or another is a great way of staying in touch with each other and what's going on and it has enhanced the life of many and re-established lost friendships, but don't rely on it.

Use it to arrange events, meetings and personal contact with people.

## Switch your phone off at 10pm

This is a tough one for many people, but it is in here for a reason. It puts you back in control of communication in your life.

What did we do before mobile phones?

It is still considered polite etiquette to not disturb people between 10pm and 8am, but it is up to you to abide by and enforce that etiquette in your life; boundaries. It will feel uncomfortable initially, you will feel you are missing out on something or something might happen and you won't know. There isn't much that can't wait until the next morning and after the initial period of adjustment to the new routine, you will feel a new freedom from the constant stress of intrusive communication.

The same principles apply to going out and leaving your phone behind – go for a walk or a run or perhaps go to the cinema and leave your mobile at home, it is very liberating.

## Reconnect

Select one person you haven't physically spoken to for a few weeks, months or years, pick up the phone and call someone today for a chat and notice how good you feel afterwards. You can also be pleased that you have brought joy into their life too, they will feel better for your call (but don't complain about your problems or talk about depression, stay off negative subjects, if you're stuck about what to say, ask them about their life).

You will learn later in this book why we feel better for having personal contact with people. It takes a bit more effort but the physiological rewards of doing so are the 'eat your greens' part of the depression diet.

> Start your depression diet today.

# Chapter 5 – False Beliefs About Depression

I want to bring you back for a moment to part of the statement from WebMD.com that said

".... people with depression sometimes fail to realize **(or accept)** that **there is a biological cause** to their depressed moods. As a result, they may **search endlessly for external causes.**"

It is my experience after over 6000 clinical hours of working with people who have depression and my own experience with depression that this is most certainly true from several perspectives:-

## 'Searching endlessly for external causes'

Unfortunately the culture around depression seems to have created a 'detachment' from the condition that leads to a failure to take responsibility for one's own thoughts and actions that are causing the depression.

The statement in itself 'living with depression' implies that there is some other entity that has moved in and you have no control to evict it – detachment from responsibility.

At the initial consultation with a new client with depression, invariably that person will explain they've either been diagnosed with depression or have depression and then go on to list all the reasons why they think that is.

**Things to blame:-**

"It's hereditary"

"My partner left/my relationship broke down"

"I lost my job, I hate my job, I can't get a job"

Someone died, followed by someone else being ill, followed by another stressful situation…

And so on. In my case, my blame was my own feelings of failure, I was struggling to bring in a big contract at work, I didn't know what to try next and I believed I was going to fail and everyone would think I was rubbish at my job.

Apart from it's hereditary, these are all events, and yes they are tough things to deal with, but does everyone who encounters these events have depression? No!

## Depression Detachment

I had a conversation via social media recently with a woman who had as her profile 'living with depression', she actually ran a support group called Living with Depression, and I asked her rather directly:-

*"Why do you choose to live with depression?"*

Of course, predictably and understandably, she came back to me saying

*"I don't choose to live with it, I have to!"*

*"Why?" I asked "Do you know it's the way you think that is causing the depression?"*

*"What do you mean?" she replied*

*I said "It's the negative thought patterns, negatively introspecting about yourself, your life and the past that's creating the condition and the lack of serotonin."*

*She said "I do have negative thoughts, I admit, but I can't get them out of my head, that's the depression. When I'm alone especially, negative voices in my mind just go round and round, they intrude my thinking and invade my thoughts, I find it difficult to get rid of them"*

*I asked her "Whose voices are they?"*

*"It's my voice," she said*

*"And you can get rid of them at times," I replied*

*"Yes", she said, "when I'm busy doing something."*

*I said to her:-*

*"So they are your thoughts and you can get rid of them at times? It is your brain, they are your thoughts, you're creating them with your imagination and believing them?"*

This is what I mean by the damaging statement 'living with depression' and the detachment from responsibility of doing anything about it – if you blame something or someone else for the cause, then paradoxically you are creating your own living reality and depression.

## Identity Crisis

This may seem contradictory to the point above about detachment from responsibility and perhaps it is; it is possible that some people believe the depression is an external force whilst others believe it is part of who they are – maybe you can do both

Some people who resign themselves to living with depression believe it is part of their personality, their make up, "it's just who I am", typical with people who see themselves as a 'glass half empty' type of person.

Depression is not part of your personality, it is an illness, one that you can be cured of if you choose. It can be a chronic illness, chronic meaning 'long term', not seriously bad, in fact in medical terms 'chronic' has been changed to 'persistent' as a more easily understood definition.

## Pity Party

Unfortunately depression is a self perpetuating condition, the more you focus on how bad you feel, the worse it gets and the worse you feel, then you focus on it even more, you talk to people and they help you focus on it – it's a downhill vicious spiral.

From a neurological point of view, in doing this you are building and strengthening neural networks in your brain that reinforce this negative thinking and behaviour.

Every time you think about past events or talk about how bad you feel you are replaying a video in your mind. A thought is not just a thought, it's a 5D video that involves all your senses, what you saw, smelt, tasted, heard and felt and this is exactly the same for imagined events, you will have associations with your senses to imaginary problems as well based on past experiences.

Think of the first (and perhaps only) time you have accidentally drunk sour milk – yuk!

Now examine what happened in your mind when I asked you to do that, did you get an image of yourself drinking it, did you get a feeling in the pit of your stomach of disgust or nausea like I did, did you smell the milk?

The opposite is also true, if you think of a great time in your life (yes I know that's hard, you've got depression, but there will be some good times), does a smile come to you lips, a picture associated with it, the sounds around you at the time?

Of course they will vary from person to person and some senses will be stronger than others, but we will all get a video.

A memory or an imagined event is not just a picture and every time you recall it, either to yourself or to tell someone else, you are reliving and reinforcing those miserable feelings.

Now, why did I start this section with pity party? Warning, you're not going to like this bit...

Well, people with depression negatively introspect about themselves, their situation or their past, often in a self pitying way – this is not helpful.

In addition, they will tell everyone who cares to listen, recalling the video and reinforcing it again and again. Well meaning, but misguided friends and relatives can inadvertently buy into this pity party, sympathise and encourage you to tell them just how awful it is and every time you see them you go through the same ritual of misery telling.

Having depression is unfortunate in that other people want to be with people who are happy, calm and enthusiastic about life. Depressed people are difficult to be with, they're hard work and bring the people down around them, so eventually they push people away. Then they are upset or angry that their 'friends' don't invite them out or seem to have deserted them – they blame their friends for the lack of contact without realising that they've been withdrawing from the world.

This is one area where I strongly and perhaps controversially disagree with the some of the advice available about how to overcome depression. It promotes a combination of three main things, which I do totally agree with;-

- Antidepressant medication
- Therapy
- Self Help

It's the second point that I have an issue with. While therapy is a helpful part of recovery, choosing an appropriate therapy will make the difference between whether you recover in a few months or 5 years from now. Some talking therapies that encourage you to look into the problems DO NOT help, you will be in therapy for years. The solution is NOT in the problem, it never is, and from a practical point of view, why pay someone to listen to your problems when you are telling anyone who will still listen anyway and going over it in your head again and again? You're very good at thinking and talking about the problem, that's NOT where you need help.

The therapy should be solution focused not problem centric. You might eventually get better with problem centric therapy, but it will take years and can even prolong the depression, opening many cans of worms along the way, looking for reasons and things to blame. The websites that recommend these therapies do actually say that 'sometimes the depression can get worse initially' – that's because it's not the RIGHT therapy. No therapy should make you feel worse before you get better, that is NOT acceptable. If you have depression and you are looking for a therapy, look for a Solution Focused Brief Therapy – this usually takes up to approximately 3 months, sometimes a bit more or less, but you will not be in therapy for years and should not be.

What problem centric therapies fail to understand and update with the recent discoveries of how the brain operates is that going over and over the problem reinforces it.

In Part 2 we go into depth about how these neural networks are formed and what you can do to create and reinforce new positive neural pathways so the old ones fade away with non-use.

## You Are What You Think and Believe

A diagnosis of depression is helpful in that it's a relief that there's an explanation for how you're feeling and it points in the direction of effective treatments, however, this can be a double edged sword.

Labels are disempowering for someone who does not understand the condition or has preconceived ideas about depression - and there is a lot of misunderstanding around depression. As this culture of 'living with depression' has grown, being given the label by someone in authority (or yourself) can be an opt out of doing anything about it.

One of the first clients I had as a trainee hypnotherapist many years ago, sat down in my clinic and proudly announced "I've been diagnosed with having a co-morbid condition". "Well done," I said, "do you want to tell me about it?"

It was almost as if it was a challenge to me 'I have this thing, I bet you can't cure me'. What she didn't realised is that it wasn't up to me to cure her, it wasn't my responsibility, it was hers, I was there to help point her in the right direction, but I couldn't do it for her.

A lady I connected with recently, Philippa, gave me a fascinating insight into her depression and a useful analogy about how she now sees it that I would like to share with you.

> *"Neuroscience teaches us that the primitive brain – the part that takes control in times of stress and creates and continues a state of depression,*

*shutdown, inertia, uncommunicative misery, is NOT an aspect of our true personality. It is a hard-wired process which over-rides the personality and is simply reacting in its primitive way to its perception of danger.'*

*I 'got' this when I read it in Emma's ebook 'Living with Depression is Rubbish', but didn't follow the thought process through to its natural conclusion until now. Because of my lifelong problem with depression I've constructed a perception of myself which includes a lot of negative stuff about the times when I've been overcome by it and it's blighted my relationships with other people. I can think of countless family gatherings and social occasions when I've been withdrawn and unable to even talk normally, let alone join in with humour or lightness, and in particular completely unable to deal with any boisterous person who drew everyone's attention to my low mood in a rude way and tried to force me to 'lighten up' (I am thinking of one particular person here, whose behaviour has since been recognised as unacceptable).*

*Sometimes people have told me outright that their friends/family thought I was rude, aloof and unsociable because of my depressed behaviour, but of course you don't need an outsider to point this out – you know at the time that you're falling short of expectations and it just reinforces the idea that you're a failure, that people don't like you, that you are forever destined to be isolated and misunderstood because of the depression you suffer.*

*The lightbulb moment this morning came when I was thinking of the nice social occasions I've had in the last week or so, when I have not been depressed, and the penny dropped that people really like the real me. And these are people that I like and admire and want to think I have lots in common with. Therefore the person I am when not overcome by depression is likeable. And the depression is a product of the primitive brain, not the real me. Therefore I don't need to judge myself harshly by the way I've been when depressed. I am allowed to enjoy the fact that my true personality is OK, I don't have to feel flawed and damaged and below standard any more.*

*This may all sound very long-winded and taking a long time to state the obvious but something very important has just become scientifically clear to me. The depression is NOT a part of my personality, it is a separate force. Therefore I don't have to try to incorporate it into my overall perception of myself, I need to completely separate it and disregard it.*

*Maybe I could make the analogy of my style in dress – which may sound superficial, but clothes are very important to me. I know I dress well and people often admire my clothes and say I look nice. Well, supposing I'm caught in a storm and find a dreadful, frumpy old raincoat dumped somewhere and put it on because I have nothing else to wear. I turn up to meet people wearing this thing and I look nothing like my usual stylish self. Friends would wonder what was wrong with me and strangers would see me as dowdy and unattractive.*

*But I can take the horrible coat off and underneath it I'm wearing a gorgeous dress which I chose for myself because it suits me. The raincoat is not part of my wardrobe and luckily the weather improves and I can throw it into a rubbish bin. I don't have any regret about doing this because it's not mine. It was a temporary reaction to a temporary problem and I have no attachment to it whatsoever.*

*I can continue the analogy, The raincoat is horrible because it was made by someone with poor skills and is not designed in any way to look nice or complement other clothing. Its only purpose is to protect whatever is underneath, regardless of what that is. And it serves that purpose perfectly. However once the storm is past it has no value or meaning at all.*

*In the past I have had some attachment to depression because I perceived it as part of my personality. I thought I had to see myself as a depressed person. Now I suddenly realise that this is not scientifically true and it is amazing. I have tears in my eyes as I type this. It is a quantum leap in my brain! Once this idea becomes a true thought pattern – which I know may take time as the opposite view has been ingrained in me for so long – it can be really transformative. I'm going to brand my negative thoughts and tendency to fall into bad thought patterns as 'the nasty old raincoat' and remember that they're not mine and I don't have to wear them.*

*It's early days I know, but this new understanding of something I thought was a permanent, integrated part of me is really empowering. I had tried anti-depressant medication in the past but it didn't feel right – it was like an emotional painkiller. Even though I was relieved of the day to day anguish, I knew all the bad feelings and thought patterns were still there underneath and my brain was just being tricked into not engaging with them. More worryingly, I seemed to have lost an important part of my rational brain as well – I made bad decisions and behaved recklessly, and was unable to process the results properly as my brain refused to acknowledge what I now know were genuine and important warning signals.*

*My heartfelt instinct was that somehow the answer lay in working with the brain as it really is, not messing it around with pharmaceutical drugs. I just didn't know how this could happen and felt completely stuck and in despair. Now I'm beginning to understand that I can learn that ability, and it is already getting results. It makes sense to me rationally, as someone with a scientific mind, and at the same time on a purely subjective level I'm noticing myself becoming more aware of my thoughts and where they might lead me. Truly this is the most helpful process I've embarked upon after years of feeling that I was the victim of a damaged mind. Not permanently damaged now, but just shaped by bad thought habits and neurological processes – which – Eureka – I can change.*

*Onward and upward..."* Philippa

> **"The depression is NOT part of my personality"**

That's interesting isn't it?

I came across a quote recently that said:-

*'Be careful what you tell yourself – You're listening'*

That's more profound than at face value when you understand how the subconscious behaves.

When you tell yourself something, and you believe it at a subconscious level, you take away your ability to overpower it.

Think of your conscious brain (the part you actively think with, the part you are using to read or listen to this) as you for a moment, and your subconscious as an elephant. Which one is more powerful?

You are an elephant trainer, a mahout, and on the whole your subconscious elephant is happy to go along with what you ask it to do, but if your subconscious elephant saw a mouse and was frightened, how much control do you think you would have of controlling the elephant then? Your elephant would bolt at top speed and you wouldn't have any hope of getting it to think rationally about the size of the mouse compared with it.

That's exactly how your subconscious behaves when frightened and you active your flight/fight response system, but equally as important is what you are choosing to believe and take on board, and this is why labels can be disempowering.

You may think rationally that you're not going to give in, but if your subconscious believes that depression is a condition you have to 'live with', and friends and family lead you to believe that you'll have depression for the rest of your life and it can always come back - then that's what will prevail and you won't put 100% into getting over it.

You already know that if you don't believe you can do something you won't even try.

The good news is however, that you CAN change your thoughts at a subconscious level, you just have to decide and believe – they are your thoughts after all.

Take a moment to think of something you used to believe you couldn't do, but now do without thinking - or a time when you changed your mind completely about something. We all can and do change our minds frequently. So why, when it's in your best interest to do that, does it seem so hard?

Fear and fear of the unknown in particular, the feeling of helplessness and lack of energy that is the domain of depression is why.

# Chapter 6 – How Depression Develops

So let's get down to the truth behind depression and have a look at the elements of the brain we need to be concerned with – stick with this bit, it's important and not overly scientific or technical.

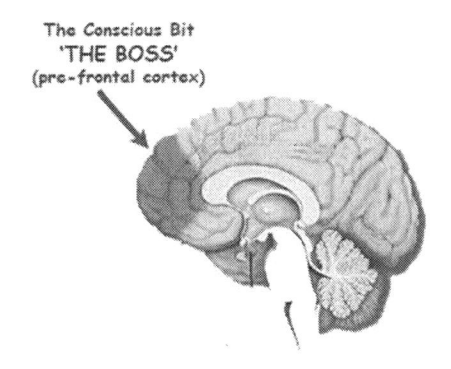

The Conscious Bit
'THE BOSS'
(pre-frontal cortex)

The first bit we need to know about is our Conscious Brain (the left pre-frontal cortex). This is the bit you use to interact with people and with the world around you, you're using that bit at the moment to read, or listen and make sense of this. We call this bit 'The Boss' and ultimately it calls the shots and makes the final decisions of which other parts it wants to collaborate with.

At the moment (because you're reading this and actively engaged in something clever) your conscious brain is working with your vast intellectual resource, your intellectual brain (or the higher cortex).

You can beat depression, this is how.

The Conscious Bit
'THE BOSS'
(pre-frontal cortex)

The Clever Bit
'YOUR EXPERTS'
(Higher Cortex)

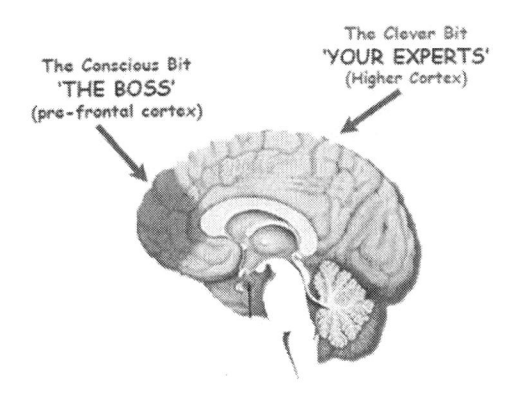

The higher cortex is split into the left and right hemispheres; the left is your logical side and the right your artistic side, you may have heard people talk about they are left or right brained. Actually, we all swap between the two regularly.

When you are working from your intellectual brain, you usually get things right in life; it will always come up answers based on a proper assessment of a situation and is generally very positive. This bit we don't share with other animals, which is why you don't see dogs driving around in cars or inventing mobile phones with keypads to suit their paws.

So far so good! We've got a conscious thinking bit that works excellently with a clever intellectual bit, rational, artistic and positive. So if we could stay here all the time, life would be pretty hunky dory wouldn't it?

But there's another bit and this is our primitive bit.

This is the original bit, well to tell the truth, is the second bit to evolve, before that was the reptilian brain, but we don't need to be concerned with that just now. The primitive bit we're talking about here is technically the Limbic system, our mammalian brain that we do share with animals.

The central and influential part of this is the Amygdala, the bit that we refer to as the flight/fight centre and this works very closely with two other primitive parts, the hippocampus which holds our primitive, and sometimes inappropriate behavior patterns or behaviours and then there's the hypothalamus which regulates the chemical responses in our body and mind.

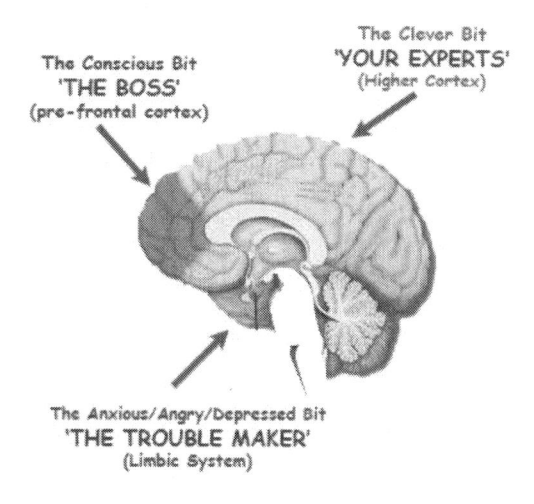

The Conscious Bit
'THE BOSS'
(pre-frontal cortex)

The Clever Bit
'YOUR EXPERTS'
(Higher Cortex)

The Anxious/Angry/Depressed Bit
'THE TROUBLE MAKER'
(Limbic System)

Now we have the boss, the clever bit and the primitive bit and it's this final part that causes people with depression so much trouble.

So, how do they interact with each other? Lets put it in perspective:-

Imagine that you went outside the house and there was a sabre tooth tiger in the street, what would happen?

Well, your heart rate would go up, your stomach would start churning, you would get all sweaty and you would be off like a shot. You would have moved from your intellectual brain to your primitive brain

This happens so quickly, it wouldn't register in your conscious brain immediately and you wouldn't want it to, you're not going to stay alive long if you're standing around in the street having a conscious conflab with your intellect asking "Golly Gosh, is that a dangerous sabre tooth tiger I see charging towards me, what's that doing here?" no doubt you would be a tasty tiger snack.

When your primitive brain steps and takes control, it does so very firmly and you are compelled into action without thinking.

This is entirely appropriate for sabre tooth tigers and you would be pleased, but the same thing tends to happen in modern life; when your anxiety levels go up - and it can be a gradual process - you lose intellectual control and, to a greater or lesser extent, the primitive brain steps in and takes control.

Your primitive brain always works within the parameters of

**Anxiety, Depression and Anger**

Or a combination of all three - we're actually very good at doing all three simultaneously.

Anxiety, depression and anger are all primitive opt out clauses, which would have been appropriate back in those primitive times, it was a dangerous world. If you had been out in the jungle hunting or picking berries or doing whatever you did in jungles in those times, there would be danger all around and I doubt you would be far away from your panic button at any given moment. And if you couldn't go out because there was snow or ice or danger outside your cave, you would probably go back inside the cave, pull a rug over your head and not interact with the world until the situation changed – this is often how we react with depression.

Anger is just a primitive way of increasing our strength so we can fend off wild animals or other wild tribesmen/women.

So, whenever your primitive brain thinks that there is some sort of crisis, emergency or danger it steps in and reacts in this way.

But there's more, when your primitive brain takes control, it behaves in certain ways:-

- It always looks at the worst possible scenario – appropriate for sabre tooth tigers, you're not going to assume it's already eaten down the street and couldn't manage another morsel, of course you're not, you are going to assume it will attack you. But we will do the same thing if we're facing redundancy, a unexpected bill has arrived or we've

had an argument perhaps, we'll jump to the worst possible scenario.
- It's also very vigilant, it's not going to let you forget there is a sabre tooth tiger outside, it will keep reminding you, so although you can distract yourself with something else temporarily, when you stop, it will bring your attention back to your problems.
- It is very obsessive, when you get something on your primitive mind, it will obsess, going over and over the details and hijacking your imagination in the process.

But this primitive brain is NOT an intellect, it can't work out what to do about a situation, it can't come up with solutions, all it can do is refer to previous patterns of behaviour. If, whatever you did yesterday, or last time you invoked the same feelings or circumstances and you survived, you will be compelled to do the same thing again. This is where, as things get more extreme and embedded in the primitive brain, people develop habits, OCD, behavioral disorders, rituals etc or, common in depression, withdraw from the world, retreat into your cave, pull the duvet over your head and push the world and problems away.

The primitive brain's primary function is survival, so it will look at everything in terms of how it applies to you and it will make everything about **you**. It becomes paranoid about other people and what they're thinking and it makes assumptions that other people are thinking negatively about you.

It thinks in terms of all or nothing. It comes from a time of kill or be killed, eat or be eaten, so to this brain, there is no grey area in the middle so it will tend to think – this **always** happens to me, I've tried **everything, nothing** works, why are the lights **always** red when I'm late for work, I'm **always** the one to apologise, you **never** say you're sorry, etc   None of that is true of course, but this primitive brain looks at the negative and makes it into an all or nothing situation.

This is important because while you are locked in your primitive brain, looking at everything in a negative light, suspicious of everything and everyone, your intellect is not able to work out solutions and you become more and more obsessed about the problems.

This part of your brain cares only about is keeping you alive, it's not rational, it doesn't care if the behaviour is appropriate or even makes any sense to your intellectual brain, if it keeps you alive, then it's done the right thing and it will make you do it again next time.

Smoking is a particularly good example of this in action.  A smoker will often associated their smoking habit with alleviating stress (it doesn't by the way, it's a stimulant, it increases anxiety, not reduces it), but we were first introduced to the propaganda of smoking helping stress in the first world war and smokers still believe it.  What really happens is, when the smokers' anxiety or stress levels rise, their primitive brain steps in and they lose intellectual control.  This then refers to the hippocampus and asks 'we've got stress, what do we do?'  The hippocampus refers to its database of survival tactics compares it with the current stress level and it replies 'Oh, we smoke a cigarette', the smoker receive a signal in the form of a craving, they smoke and they survive.  The hippocampus puts a tick in the box because once again it has advised correctly, its human has survived, therefore the strategy works and must be correct.

Intellectually, everyone knows that smoking does not help you stay alive and it is not a clever survival tactic, in fact all the evidence points to the opposite, but we don't smoke from our clever, rational, intellectual brain. We smoke from the primitive brain, it's a habit stored in the hippocampus.

So, to clarify when your anxiety levels go up, the primitive reactionary brain takes over and tells you what to do, even if that's withdrawing from the world and staying in bed.

Which begs the question of course, why do your anxiety levels go up?

Well, it's not circumstances or events in your life which cause anxiety - if it was every student at university would be having panic attacks and they're not all having panic attacks, so we know it is not events.

It is your thought patterns surrounding events.

The primitive brain is a negative brain and it will negatively forecast the future which could be big things, like 'I'll never get that job' or I'll never get married or have children', or 'I'll never get out of this financial predicament', but equally, it can be everyday things – 'that will never work for me', 'I never get the opportunities', 'my partner's going to come home in a bad mood', 'fighting depression is hard', 'I'll never be free of depression', 'I'm going to have to live with this for the rest of my life' "nothing will ever work' – you get the gist of it!

Someone who is operating from their primitive brain will be negatively thinking about just about everything, often without realising.

*People who negatively introspect about themselves, their life or the past have a tendency towards depression, those who negatively forecast the future lean towards anxiety – but we can do both, and frequently do. It's your personality type and the influences as you grew up, and around you now that will determine whether you go into anxiety, depression or anger or jump around all three.*

Consider this as an example: - You have been called into a meeting with your boss. But you're stressed, so you start negatively forecasting what the meeting is about and immediately think the worst and make a mental leap to the worst possible scenario. As the meeting gets closer, you go over and over it in your mind, you go over it fifty times and, fifty times, it's going to be a disaster, there's a problem or you're going to get made redundant or whatever other disastrous conclusion you can imagine.

The meeting goes OK, they generally do, but by this time you've been through it 51 times, 50 times in your head. And what is really important to understand here is that your brain does not know the difference between imagination and reality. It is YOUR brain, it only knows what information you give it, what you think, what you learn and choose to believe, but also what you imagine.

So, when you negatively forecast the future, imagining something is going to happen or go wrong, your brain doesn't know the difference between that and a sabre tooth tiger, it just interprets the negative forecasting it as crisis, emergency or danger and steps in and takes control.

When you negatively introspect about the past, your life or yourself your subconscious brain doesn't understand time in the same way your conscious brain does.

Every time you ruminate about something negative in your life, you recall the feelings you had at that time in your mind so again your primitive brain interprets it as a crisis, emergency or danger and you reinforce the negative feelings and emotions.

Then it does the risk assessments and imagines everything else which could go wrong, focusing on everything in negative terms It will look for threat or danger everywhere, in work or outside, in your relationships, how other people might be thinking about you - and the more you do it, the more you get locked in.

## The Default Mode Network

The problem for us humans is that our default operating system, or the part of our brain that we default to when it's not actively engaged in something positive, is this primitive survival bit.

This is the reason why we have survived so long and evolved, if our default was positive, always looking at the bright side, we wouldn't have survived very long at all. If we were skipping along in the jungle and there was a dark shadow in the undergrowth, it is good for survival to assume its sabre tooth tiger and not a rock. If it was a rock and we assumed the sabre tooth, then the consequences are just feeling a little bit stupid perhaps, but the other way round – yummy, lunch for said sabre tooth!

So, in primitive times, we were perfectly functioning, evolving and, most importantly of all, surviving humans.

But where are the sabre tooth's today? They're not in your back garden and they're not down the street or in Tesco's either. We no longer live in primitive times. Humans have become top predator in most circumstances, but our brain, instead of updating itself, has applied the same primitive principles to modern life.

Today our perceived dangers are more likely to be health, money, materialistic possessions and relationships, rather than angry tigers on the loose. Our primitive brain still interprets the feelings of anxiety or worry as crisis or danger, just as it did two hundred thousand years ago, but where do those feelings come from?

The answer lies in our thoughts – it is not the situation, but **how we are thinking about** the situation.

> **How we think determines how we feel and**
>
> **how we feel determines how we behave.**

or

## **Negative forecasting = negative feelings = negative action or reaction.**

Understanding this concept of the negative thinking primitive brain vs the positive solution thinking intellect is central to taking control and directing your thoughts in a positive way to reverse depression.

People who think they are a 'glass half empty' unlucky soul have unleashed the power of their primitive brain – are these people super successful enjoying life to the full, living life on their terms?  Doubtful.

More likely they are looking for reasons for their misery, blaming every other man and his dog for his poor luck, smoking, (do your own research – how many highly successful people smoke?) disassociating themself from any responsibility, wondering why they can't hold down a job or never get promoted, why friends don't invite them out any more or come round, why they can't afford this or that – it's not their fault, it's everyone else's and the world owes them.

It is this negative thinking about the future or negatively introspecting about yourself, your life, circumstances or your past that is converted into ANXIETY which we store up in what we call the STRESS BUCKET.

We're going to understand more about the Stress Bucket in later chapters, but before we do, I think it's important to become more aware of what is 'negative thinking'.  You might think you know what that is, but do you really?

# Chapter 7 – What is Negative Thinking?

## Attitude and Awareness.

Your attitude to life will play an important role in your subconscious thought patterns and why you are depressed.

Change your attitude to life and you will change your life.

Negative thinking is fundamental to what has gone wrong, why you are depressed and what needs to change for you to become happy, joyful, motivated and full of energy.

Many people live in denial or ignorance of how they are actually thinking. Most don't give it a thought, it's just them, and some disassociate themselves from their thoughts – 'I've got these horrible thoughts going around in my head all the time'. Before you can begin the process of climbing out of that black cloud of depression, you need to become aware of how you are thinking at a subconscious level and how this not only affects your mental health but influences your life as well.

Let me give you an example of how we can be unaware of how negative thinking, at a subconscious level, influences our life.

Someone I know, who genuinely believes he is a positive person, has a motto taught to him by his grandfather and he likes to tell other people he lives by it and it goes like this:-

*"Don't do to other people what you don't want others to do to you"*

Seems fair enough, right?

But lets have a closer look at that statement and the quote from the Bible (Luke 6:13) it's been adapted from which is:-

"Do unto others as you would have them do unto you"

On the surface, both statements appear similar, but the first one is full of negative subconscious language whereas the second is entirely positive – can you see the difference?

This person I know quite well and he does suffer from bouts of depression and anger.

There was a post on Facebook this week from someone in a group I was browsing that said

*"I know 97% of people will not even bother to read this, but ...."*

That is a classic example of negative forecasting of the future and a good demonstration of false beliefs – take a closer look:-

'I know 97% of people' - He doesn't 'know' and 97% is an entirely made-up statistic. He believes it though and sadly could have possibly made it come true because, if you're like me, it puts you off reading the rest of the statement.

What do you think would have happened if he had put something positive like

"97% of people who read this are going to ....."

Quite possibly curiosity will cause you to stop and read a bit more.

Subconscious language patterns influence what happens in your life.

Particular self sabotaging statements to be very wary of include;-

*"I can't because"*

Believe you 'can't' do something is a poor start, but then justify it with an excuse and you will influence your destiny in that direction without a doubt because you wont even try, believing before you start that trying is a waste of time.

*"I can't do any more"*

*"I can't continue"*

Both similar to the first one. You know that backed into a corner or when something is important enough to you, you can and you will do more; you can and you will continue. If you have no choice, then you do.

Starting now, switch those statements to begin with

"How can I"

Another typically self sabotaging statement people use frequently is:-

"The problem is..."

This statement is an instant give away that you're operating from your primitive negative brain. This part of the brain focuses on problems. Focusing on the problems causes anxiety, which activates the flight/fight responses.

Deliberately focusing on finding solutions will engage the intellectual brain and give it a positive instruction of what you need to find answers for.

You need to start giving your intellectual brain something to do. It can't act on something NOT to do, you need to think in terms of positive instruction.

Imagine for a moment that you are the supervisor of staff in your office. Are you going to give instructions of what you DON'T want them to do that day - Jack, you shouldn't follow up on the sales enquiries today, Jane, don't write the report on profit and loss, John, you can't get quotes for the new computer system.

If you tell them what they can't do and don't give any instruction of what you do need or require, a purpose or direction – what is going to happen to them and the company do you think?

If I ask you to NOT think of a pink elephant – what has popped into your head?

And if I ask you to NOT think of that pink elephant that is NOT chasing a blue elephant around in circles….

What are you thinking about now?

In this same way you can't tell yourself not to worry about something, your brain can't do anything with a negative instruction, it needs positive direction of what to do.

Other forms of negative thinking we're not always aware of are:

## Criticism

Are you aware you're subconsciously criticising yourself, other people or things? A friend of mine, who would also swear blind that she's a positive person, narrates the TV in a commentary of criticism. Say, for example, the news comes on, she might start with a comment about the newsreader – 'that colour doesn't suit her' or 'isn't she looking thin' or perhaps 'she's put on weight'. She will continue making comments about every news item and they are always negative. She criticises her neighbours, her family, the packaging on products, the roads, the post office, young people today – well you get the picture. Criticism is always negative and never necessary.

If something needs correcting, there are positive ways of giving feedback without making someone feel bad about it.

However, being critical of others or things reveals the underlying negative thinking.

## Negatively introspecting about yourself and your life

Beating yourself up or being critical about yourself not only lowers your self-esteem and destroys your confidence; it makes you feel pretty miserable in the process.

What good does it do? Nothing,

When I worked for a brief period in education many people in the college I worked with complained about their job and the college endlessly. If you don't like something change it. If you choose to stay in it, find solutions; complaining about it without doing anything will bring yourself and everyone around you down and is completely pointless. You may not be able to change the job or the organisation, but you can change your attitude towards them, it is simply a choice.

## Negatively introspecting about the past

You can't change the past. Stop it.

Holding on to guilt only affects you. Stop it.

## Negative Imagination about other people's thoughts

This is massively common. Remember I said that humans can't cope with ambiguity, with not knowing? Well, we don't know what other people are thinking – ever. So we make it up!

People use their imagination to try and work out what someone else is thinking and if, when you are in a negative primitive brain place, you will think the worst and what's more, you will believe it.

You don't know what someone else is thinking, so if this is a habit of yours, either ask the person about it or accept that you don't know. Don't make it up and believe it to be true.

## Focusing on the problems in your life.

When you worry about problems you are causing anxiety. As your anxiety levels rise, your primitive brain steps in and compels you to focus on the problems even more. You obsess about them, they go round and round in your head, your imagination takes over and you imagine all the worst possible scenarios and you identify all the things you can't do because …. Sound familiar? Where is this actually getting you – nowhere except deeper into depression.

Focusing on problems is not going to solve them. Finding solutions will.

OK, so thinking about problems is quite a natural 'go to' when you've got problems and, as I explained telling you to NOT think about problems is as good as telling you to NOT think about pink elephants, but sit tight because we're about to move on to what you CAN do instead.

## Overthinking

Before we do however, I want a quick word about overthinking – stop it!

You will be pleased to learn that, on the whole, it is people with a good cognitive ability (intelligent) that get anxiety and depression because they 'overthink' situations and events. Unfortunately when in depression this is in a negative context, which only reinforces and deepens the depression, but nonetheless if you weren't an intelligent person you probably wouldn't have depression.

The good news is however, that being the intelligent person you are, that clever brain of yours can work equally as hard to get you out of the depression as it did to get you into it in the first place.

# Chapter 8 – The Stress Bucket

I appreciate you are probably keen to move on to what you need to do to get out of depression, before we do, there are a couple more highly relevant things you need to learn so when you put it all together, climbing out of the black cloud of depression will be easy.

One of those things is the 'stress bucket'

As we go about our day, we fill up the stress bucket if we're prone to think in a negative way, we will fill up our stress bucket quickly until we get to 'max fill level' a bit like your kettle.

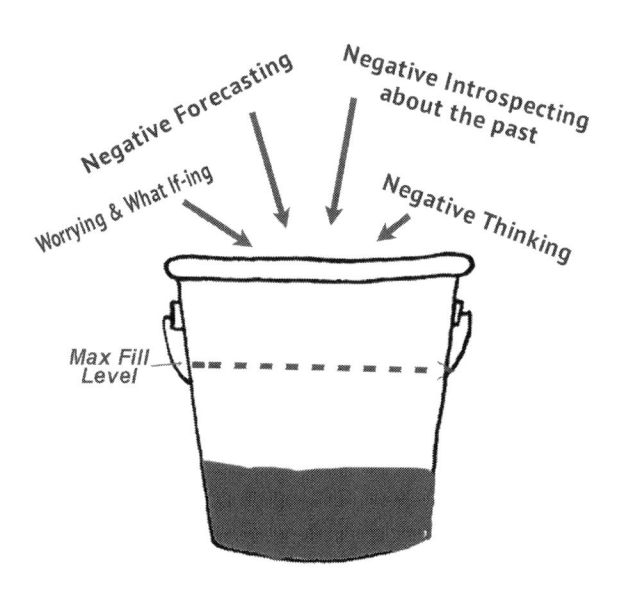

You can beat depression, this is how.

You're generally OK as long as you keep below the max fill level, but put too much in and this is what causes you to lose intellectual control and to a greater or lesser extent your primitive brain steps in and takes over

How much you are keeping in your stress bucket will have a direct correlation to how much your primitive brain is in control.

Left unchecked, and if nothing changes in your life, eventually your stress bucket overflows and your primitive brain steps in taking some sort of physical action to stop you doing whatever it thinks is creating the danger. Some people start having panic attacks or develop physical illnesses. Others 'shut down' mentally and just can't cope any more – this often happens with depression.

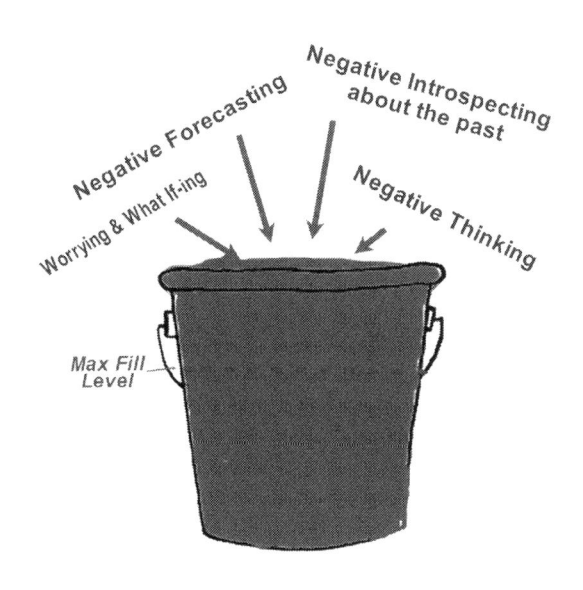

*Negative Forecasting*
*Worrying & What If-ing*
*Negative Introspecting about the past*
*Negative Thinking*

Max Fill Level

When my stress bucket overflowed in 2002, I didn't understand what was happening at the time, but I still remember it vividly.

I was working for a well known international electronics company at the time in IT sales; I was working on a project involved with computerising the NHS and as my customers were located all over the UK, I worked from home. When I wasn't travelling to meetings, I worked from my home office.

I was under a lot of pressure from my company and the stress had been building for a while, but I didn't realise how bad it had become – ie I didn't know my stress bucket was about to overflow.

One day I got up as normal, got dressed for work and sat in my home office in front of my computer and I just stared at it. When the phone rang. I had a surge of anxiety and just stared at it - I couldn't answer the phone. I was shutting down mentally.

I managed to do the minimum possible which was to answer emails from my boss and send him a question around 9am as a signal that I was working. But I wasn't really, I wasn't thinking about anything much except worrying that I should be doing something, couldn't and would get found out and I would be sacked.

This went on for several weeks, I would get up at the normal time, get dressed and sit in front of my computer staring at it and I would stay there all day until 5pm. I wasn't skiving, I wasn't outside in the garden or doing the washing or watching TV, I just sat there numb.

Eventually, after being persuaded by a friend who could tell there was something wrong, I went to the doctor. I remember I just sat there and cried, I could hardly get the words out and didn't know what to say because there was nothing physically wrong with me and I felt stupid. She immediately signed me off with stress for two weeks. (she wrote virus on the sick note).

I remember it was such a relief I wouldn't have to face work for two whole weeks, but the thoughts lingered in the background, what was I going to do after that.

The company called me in to see the company doctor – he took one look at me and said:

*"you have depression, you should be on antidepressants"*

I went into denial immediately,

*"I don't have depression, it's work related stress – this job has caused me stress, I don't need antidepressants,"* I angrily protested.

All in all I was signed off work for three months, the thought of going back to the same job and facing what I perceived to be getting worse in my absence, with my boss being angry that I had been off for so long had me relapsing every time (this thinking was all made up in my imagination).

The day I started getting better was the day I handed in my resignation – I didn't know what I was going to do, it meant leaving a six-figure salary job, I had no idea how I was going to survive and pay the mortgage, but I would deal with that, anything was better than feeling like this any longer.

Now with hindsight and the training in psychology, neurology and solution focused therapy I understand exactly why it happened, how I created it and why I started to get better the day I made a decision to do something different and make changes in my life and I will explain it all in Part 2.

Back to the stress bucket…

We all need a certain amount of positive stress in our lives to motivate us and get us out of bed in the morning, but as depression develops and deepens, we get locked into patterns of negative thinking constantly filling up the stress bucket.

Luckily we have a way of emptying the stress bucket naturally and we do this in REM sleep.

You may have heard of REM, Rapid Eye Movement. It is a phase of sleep we go into about every ninety minutes throughout the night. The first phase of REM is for just a few minutes, but this lengthens every phase until just before we wake up in the morning, when it's approximately 10 minutes long.

During REM we are rerunning events of the day, either in clear narrative or in metaphor; this is when we are dreaming.

Sleep is still one of the great mysteries of the mind, but there are many theories about why we do this and what is actually happening during REM. One of those theories believed by scientists is that during REM, our brain is sorting information from the day, if you like 'filing it' and diffusing it of emotion.

You already know how this works: perhaps you've had a bad day at work, someone has upset or annoyed you and you go home disturbed about it. You tell your partner or spouse and they say 'don't worry about it', but you can't stop thinking about it and it's going around and around your mind when you go to sleep at night. During in the night you move things from your emotional primitive brain to your rational intellectual brain during REM, the incident is put in perspective by your intellect and in the morning you wake up and you've forgotten all about it.

So, if this is all working properly you wake up in the morning with an empty stress bucket, completely refreshed, full of energy and ready to start the day.

But if you have depression this doesn't always happen as it should and you can end up in a state of perpetual exhaustion.

So what goes wrong?

# Chapter 9 – Why is Depression Exhausting?

As we've already seen, the over-activity of negative thinking is filling up the stress bucket to overflowing on a daily basis, which keeps the primitive brain locked in and the depressed person fixated on the negatives and problems in their life, so they are stuck in a vicious cycle.

Normally the stress bucket would be emptied at night and you wake up without anxiety or depression in the morning.

However, REM sleep is restricted to around twenty five percent of sleep in adults and for very good reason.

During the REM phase of sleep the brain is hyperactive. We tend to believe that when we fall asleep we 'shut down', reset and recuperate from the day. This isn't true, many things are going on in our sleep including cell regeneration, cleansing of toxins, repair and maintenance of our bodies and our minds.

Our mind is more active during REM than it is when we are awake. So REM is in itself is exhausting.

If you have been filling up your stress bucket to overflowing with negative thinking, your brain literally has to work overtime during REM to try and empty it.

People with depression stay in the REM phase of sleep too long, thus exhausting themselves further.

When they wake up, they are still exhausted and this encourages them to go back to sleep to attempt to empty their stress bucket again – another phase of REM, which is hard work mentally and they end up in a constant cycle of exhaustion and sleep.

Some antidepressants restrict REM sleep, or bypass it altogether to help alleviate this sleep exhaustion cycle.

Part of the overall solution to depression is to restrict and regulate your own sleep patterns.

## Exercise 2 – Normalise Sleep

Unlike insomnia where you can't always sleep on command, you can stop yourself going to sleep unnecessarily.

It's tempting and often you will be compelled to sleep, especially if you have time to do so. However, if you are in a situation where you can't just fall asleep, for example at work or out shopping, in a café or taking a walk, then you won't.

Generally you need eight hours sleep a night, some people a little more and some less, but mostly around the eight hour mark is sufficient.

Develop some strategies and tactics for yourself to restrict your sleep to no more than eight hours at night.

Don't worry, you are not going to use this exercise alone, resulting in constant exhaustion. I know you think having a nap is helping, but it's doing the opposite - perpetuating the problem.

You will be doing this in conjunction with exercises that help you to not pile so much into your stress bucket in the first place, so you're helping the depression from all angles simultaneously.

If you find you are feeling tired in the daytime find something to do:-

Go for a walk, get out of the house, change your environment, put yourself with people, pop in and see a friend or family member. Stay active.

As you will learn in Part 2, positive activity is one of the keys to curing depression, so instead of sleeping find things to do. It doesn't matter how small they are or what they are as long as you are doing something positive instead of sleeping.

## Take it one hour at a time – trick yourself into it.

I do this when I'm struggling to focusing on writing. I tell myself I'm going to write or work for just one hour, then at the end of that hour I'm invariably in the middle of a chapter or subject and I either go on without thinking or I tell myself just one more hour or even another half an hour. If you tell yourself at the beginning of the day 'right - I'm not going to sleep during the day today', it can be overwhelming and you give up before you've even started. Break it down into small chunks and be pleased with yourself every time you pass one of those milestones.

## Change your habits

If you follow the same pattern of behaviour and same order for the day you will invariably be compelled to sleep at the same times. Just because you always do something a particularly way, it doesn't mean you have to keep doing it that way. Habits feel comfortable and enjoyable quite often, but that doesn't mean you have to follow them blindly if you have developed bad habits into your routines.

Stepping Out Of The Cloud

Find a new enjoyable routine that keeps you active, with people and interested in your day.

# Chapter 10 – The Biological Cause

Back to that statement from WebMD

".... people with depression sometimes fail to realise (or accept) that there is a biological cause to their depressed moods. As a result, they may search endlessly for external causes."

So, what else makes up this biological cause?

We've discussed the neurological cause; the negative thinking and replaying the internal videos time and time again that's reinforcing the negativity, leading to your primitive brain thinking there is some sort of crisis, emergency or danger, sending you running into your proverbial cave.

Another biological cause is centered around the physiological responses of the mind and body – your chemical makeup. When you have depression, the neurotransmitters and hormones in your mind and body have become unbalanced. In particular serotonin and dopamine levels have dropped below acceptable levels, also altering the flight/fight responses to some sort of crisis, emergency or danger.

Serotonin and dopamine are essential neurotransmitters (chemical messengers) that are responsible for helping us cope with life, motivating us, helping us cope with pain, they make us braver (so we can face whatever we need to), help us cope with fear, boost our immune system, help us sleep properly and also - and perhaps most importantly - help with healthy efficient functioning of the higher cortex or intellectual part of the brain. When we have sufficient or abundant serotonin and dopamine levels we feel happy, joyful, motivated, energetic, focused etc – need I go on?

If you have depression you will recognise from these symptoms that you are lacking sufficient levels of these chemicals and your body could be looking for external substitutes (sugars & carbohydrates, nicotine, alcohol, gambling, illegal or prescription drugs).

You can understand that with a lack of these essential neurotransmitters that you find it difficult to motivate yourself or find an interest or focus in anything much. Your sleep patterns will be all over the place with some people finding it difficult to sleep whereas others are tired all the time and just want to go back to bed. Weight gain and weight loss by more than 5% are on the list of symptoms indicating depression and this is often due to increased bingeing on 'comfort foods'.

The good news however, is that you can (and should) deliberately and consciously increase the production of these wonderful feel-good neurotransmitters. When you have sufficient levels, it's easy to maintain and it is everyone's responsibility to maintain their own balance.

Sadly with or modern lifestyle of convenience, life has become so distorted from how we were originally designed to live, that some people don't naturally produce enough as part of their daily routine, but we can all learn what it is we need to do to adapt and tweak our lifestyle so this happens easily and naturally again.

I had a client recently who came to see me for depression, actually it was excessive alcohol consumption, but she also confided she was depressed. During the first part of the session, as I always do, I asked her what good things had happened this week. After a little thought she told me that one of her good things was that her cousin was coming to stay. I asked her why that was a good thing and she said "because he's always so happy, full of energy and enthusiasm for life". "Oh, and why is that," I asked, "what does he like to do?" She looked at me a little confused and I explain what I meant was what does he do in his spare time. "Oh, he likes sport" she said. "Do you like having people visit" I asked. "Oh yes", she replied.

> **Positive Activity**
>
> **Positive Interaction**
>
> **Positive thinking**

These are the three things you can do for yourself, as part of that self-help bit of the recommendations that will create serotonin and dopamine and Part 2 explains in detail what they involve.

# Part 2

## Getting 'Un-depressed'

## Creating Happiness

# Chapter 11 – Making Yourself Happy

I had a partner not so long ago who, at the start of the relationship, said to me;

*"It's my job to make you happy."*

As sweet and well intentioned as that was, in my very unromantic way I replied:

*"No it isn't, it's my job to make me happy."*

Needless to say it didn't go down too well and was probably very tactless on my part, but it is true.

Don't take my word for it. It's generally accepted that Einstein was a pretty clever guy, right? Well he said…

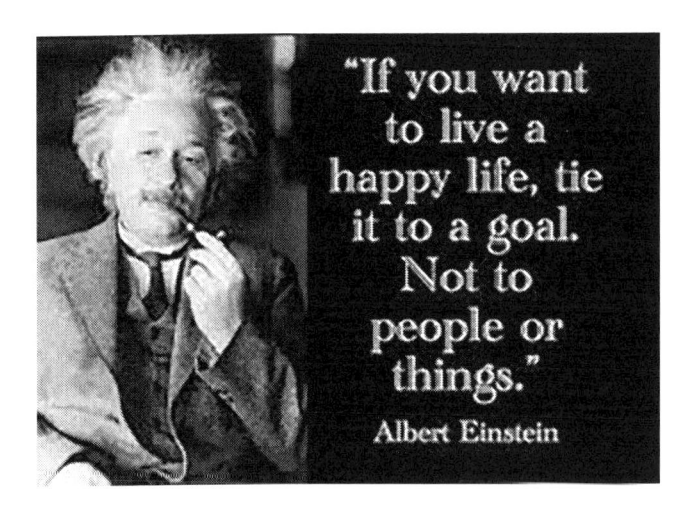

> "If you want to live a happy life, tie it to a goal. Not to people or things."
> 
> Albert Einstein

It does, scientifically, make us happy to be with other people (see Chapter 15) but our happiness is not dependent on someone or something.

There is a science to being happy that everyone can achieve and it is up to you to do the right things that create the happiness from within.

Needless to say in life 'shit happens', but its not events, people or things that cause our moods, it's how we think about them and ultimately how we deal with them.

Making YOU happy is YOUR job, its not the doctor's, your partner's or the boss' and if you have depression right now, all it means is that you haven't learned the right techniques to do that yet.

It's not your fault if you don't know, this is not something that you're taught in school. You can learn it subconsciously from parents that are happy because you will grow up mimicking the way they think, talk and behave, but if you were not that lucky and grew up in a household with depression, negativity, criticism, anxiety, stress, and anger, then that's what you will have learnt.

The good news though is that you can learn the skill of happiness quite easily and the more you practice, the more it becomes embedded in your subconscious until you just are happy.

# Chapter 12 – Stepping Out Of The Cloud

I think we've established that telling you to STOP thinking negatively or stop worrying is a complete waste of time – if you could just do that you would have done it already – right?

Over time, long before depression came knocking, you were practicing thinking in a negative way, so you will be pretty good at it by now and it will be a habit. Just dropping habits, especially something that is subtly coming from the subconscious does not always happen overnight.

One of the more common statements I hear from people with depression is that fighting it is exhausting.

From this moment forwards you are going to **stop** fighting depression, you will turn your back and walk in completely the opposite direction towards happiness step by step, and this is how you're going to do it.

Just as negative thinking is a fundamental part of what caused the depression in the first place, understanding about the physiological effects that negative thinking has on your mind and body is fundamental to turning around and climbing out of it.

# Chapter 13 – Chemical Balance

Human are 80% water, or probably more accurately, liquid because we are in actual fact a melting pot of chemicals, neurotransmitters and hormones travelling around our body through our veins in our blood and other liquids. So it stands to reason that messages travel from one part of our body to another via chemical messengers – neurotransmitters.

We are in control of that chemical balance. Every decision we make of what we consume, every thought we have and every action we do, or not do, will have an influence on this chemical mix and on determining whether we are operating on our intellectual or primitive brain.

Your emotions, feelings, motivation, energy, confidence, courage, immune system and health - in fact, every part of your life is intrinsically linked to your chemical balance and it is up to you to keep that balance at its optimum.

Your brain is the control centre for your whole body, the way you think has a hugely important influence on these chemicals and affects your body right down to a cellular level.

There is a field of science called psychoneuroimmunology that explores the relationship between how we think, the neurotransmitters we produce and the effect on our immune system. Science has also recently discovered epigenetic switches in our DNA or silent genes which can be triggered or not, depending on the individual, how they think, what they consume and their lifestyle. This means that we can have DNA with our genes for diseases such as cancer and Alzheimer's, but we don't necessarily trigger them and if you do have those genes it is not predetermined that you will get the conditions. There is a focus on research into what triggers certain genes, but if you consider the discoveries within psychoneuroimmunology about how thinking influences cells, it is even more in your interest to practice positive thinking and invest in a healthy balance of neurotransmitters.

There are many neurotransmitters and hormones, but for the purpose of understanding depression we are going to focus on just three of the most important – Serotonin, Dopamine and Adrenaline

## Serotonin

Serotonin is THE most important neurotransmitter and one of the fastest for carrying messages between brain cells and around our body and the best things about serotonin are that it makes us feel good, it motivates us, it makes us braver, it helps us cope with physical fear, it helps us cope with pain and boosts our immune system. It's our 'happy' neurotransmitter.

Going back to those ancient primitive times again serotonin was a reward for survival, for getting things right, for hunting, gathering and carrying out certain evolutionary processes – you can imagine how happy those cavemen were when they discovered fire and could sit round a camp fire and not only keep warm mid December, but could also feel safe because predators were afraid of it - I bet they felt good and doesn't it still give us a feel good vibe today sat around a camp fire with friends.

So although we don't have to go out hunting any more and we mostly have central heating, we do have to create serotonin by understanding the behaviour of our early ancestors and adapting it for our modern lifestyles.

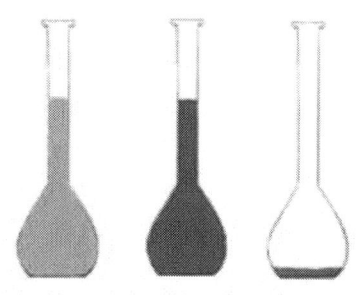

**Happy, Relaxed, Motivated, In Control**

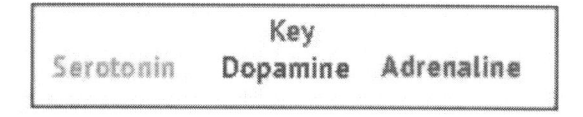

| Key | | |
|---|---|---|
| Serotonin | Dopamine | Adrenaline |

Serotonin is the chemical we need to be at our best moving through life easily and feeling happy with an abundance of energy, but what does it actually do?

Serotonin carries messages between the nerve cells in our bodies and minds and, in particular, the nerve cells in our brain or neurons.

## *Neuron*

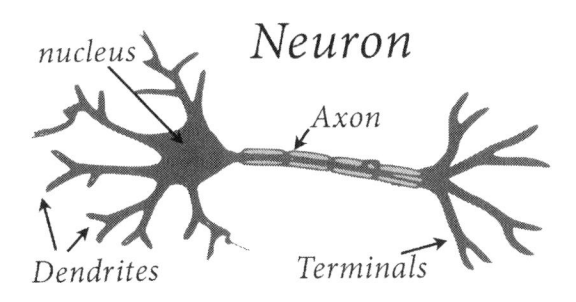

*nucleus*
*Axon*
*Dendrites*  *Terminals*

Each neuron has a 'tail' called the axon and dendrites that branch out and act as the connectors. Axons and dendrites connect to each other and together they form neural networks

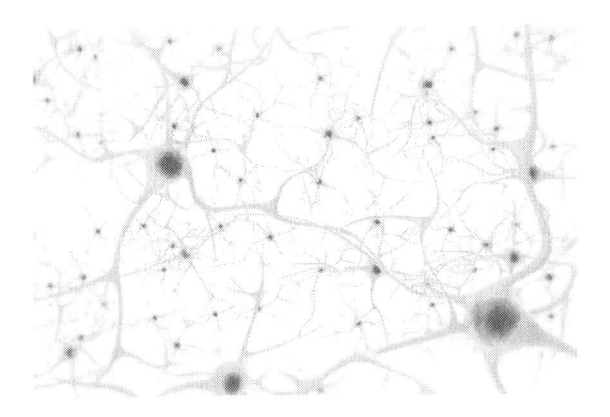

The average human adult brain has 100 billion neurons in the brain. You can't learn a skill or understand concepts, language or anything with one brain cell, you may think you know people who have just the one, but in reality we need millions, all acting as one big network to do most of the stuff we need to. But even the axons and dendrites don't physically connect, there is a small gap called the synaptic gap and something needs to bridge that gap.

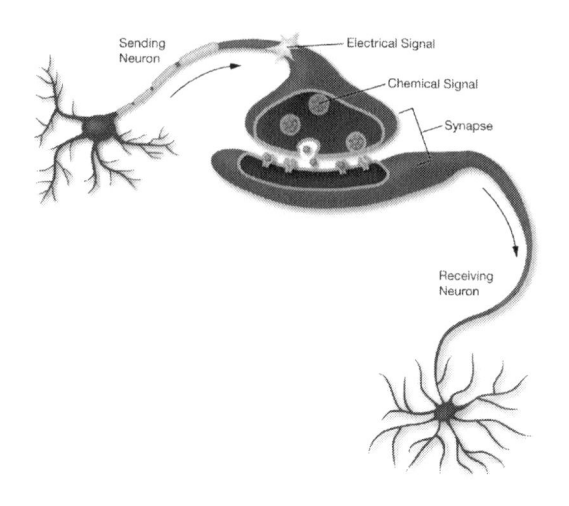

Serotonin is the substance that bridges the gap carrying the message from one neuron to the next – a neurotransmitter.

The more serotonin you have, the quicker and more efficient your neural networks function. When you have sufficient levels of serotonin, your mind is more efficient, more focused, more able to concentrate and problem-solve and you feel good.

Serotonin is the gold standard in neurotransmitters and we need to learn how to produce it if we want to cope easily with life.

## Dopamine

Dopamine is another one of the more important neurotransmitters; science is still learning about dopamine, but it is accepted that dopamine plays a major role in rewarding us for doing something good and provides the motivation to do it again, so it is closely linked to habit forming.

You can understand the role of dopamine in both survival and evolution, if as a caveman you had to go outside to hunt, but you didn't 'feel' like it or it was raining perhaps, the thought of a tasty dinosaur steak might motivate you to go out into the rain and hunt the dinosaur  - or at least the thought of dying of starvation if you didn't might be an appropriate motivator.  Then having caught said dinosaur, how good would you feel sitting around the cave fire with the family for dinosaur steak dinner?

You have survived again and your family are pleased with you and that feels good – dopamine.

Dopamine is associated with addiction (this is different from a dependency), if you are not creating enough dopamine in a healthy way, your hippocampus can make associations and connections with substances and habits that are not particularly helpful for our health and lifestyle. When you introduce and practice good reward habits that create dopamine and serotonin, the bad ones fade away, the compulsion to do something you don't really want or need to lessen.

## Adrenaline

Adrenaline is a hormone produced in the adrenal glands, which is activated by the amygdala, the influential part of your brain in the flight/fight response system.

When the amygdala is activated, the adrenal gland is quickly alerted and releases adrenaline into the blood stream causing a number of physiological changes:-

⇒ The heart rate goes up to pump blood and oxygen around the body quicker, sending more oxygen to the major muscle groups you're going to need if you're fighting or running away including your brain which needs to stay sharp and focused.
⇒ Breathing quickens to oxygenate the blood which is being pumped around the body faster.
⇒ Blood initially rushes to the surface of your skin (hence blushing). If you're going to get cut in a fight your blood needs to coagulate quickly and form a barrier against infection with the white blood cells.
⇒ Energy is redirected from systems or organs that are not necessary in the course of flight or fight – one of these is your digestive system. You do not need to be eating a sandwich or digesting dinosaur while you are fighting or fleeing from a sabre tooth tiger.

You may have noticed that when you are worrying about something, perhaps you have to go on stage or go into a situation you are anxious about, you are more likely to have nausea than hunger.

The stomach is closely involved in the autonomic nervous system (automatic reactions) and you can feel adrenaline in your stomach when you are nervous, we call it butterflies.

Adrenaline is the fastest neurotransmitter or hormone – it is responsible for your flight or fight, it literally keeps you alive by reacting before your conscious brain is even aware of potential dangers. It is faster than serotonin and will take precedence and suppress your serotonin levels. You could be sitting there right now as happy as Larry (whoever he is), but if there was a large crash or roar outside from the sabre tooth tiger, you would forget all about being happy, your flight/fight mechanism would kick in, adrenaline would flood your bloodstream and your primitive brain would step forwards to deal with the situation.

In primitive times this interaction of hormones and neurotransmitters kept us alive and evolving, but the environment and circumstances of our modern life have changed, resulting in the balance of these chemicals not being as naturally maintained as they would have been in primitive times.

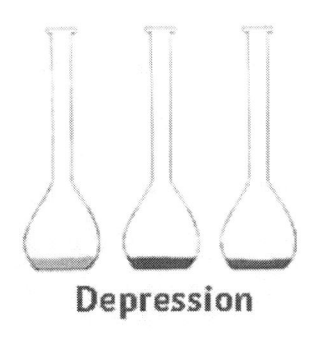

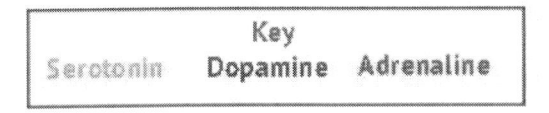

**Depression**

Key
Serotonin    Dopamine    Adrenaline

If we have not formed habits growing up that simulate the behaviour of our primitive ancestors, our chemical balance can become disrupted leading to anxiety, depression and anger.

When you have depression, your chemical balance typically looks like this

You are not producing enough neurotransmitters so you find it difficult to feel joy, think clearly, focus or concentrate when you don't have enough serotonin bridging the synaptic gaps. You will find it hard to get motivated to do anything, even the simplest of jobs, not because you're lazy, it's because your dopamine levels are not high enough to motivate you into action to get the reward of completing the task. You will find it incredibly frustrating and probably beat yourself up about it, but still seem unable to do it, however much it upsets you.

If the body cannot get enough serotonin and dopamine, it will go to substitute sources. Sugar is a serotonin substitute, so anything sweet or simple carbohydrates and starchy foods are an available substitute, but it isn't real serotonin, so the craving for it begins again shortly after you've eaten without getting motivated.

Serotonin is also known to be the off switch for appetite, so if someone doesn't have sufficient levels of serotonin, they will get food cravings and hunger and the signal to stop eating when full becomes distorted.

## Anxiety

Although it isn't the subject of this book, it's worth touching on briefly because anxiety and depression often co-exist.

You can beat depression, this is how.

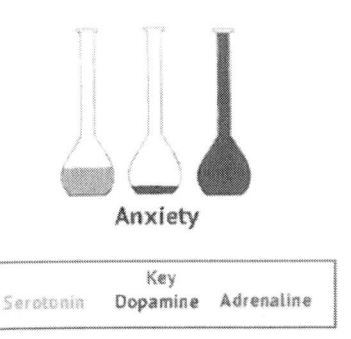

Anxiety

Key
Serotonin   Dopamine   Adrenaline

Negative forecasting of the future, worrying and 'what if-ing', creates too much adrenaline. You can have some serotonin, but it will be suppressed by the faster adrenaline in your bloodstream.

The reward motivation system becomes controlled by the adrenaline, the reward being survival instead of progress.

Your brain doesn't know the difference between imagination and reality so when you imagine negative future outcomes your brain will interpret it as real perceived danger and an appropriate chemical reaction takes place.

# Chapter 14 – What Your Doctor Doesn't Tell You About Antidepressants

There is a valid reason your doctor doesn't tell you too much about antidepressants.

If you were to make an appointment to see the doctor when you are at your lowest, desperate for some help, and your doctor gave you a list of things you needed to do to get yourself out of depression, including exercise and eat healthily, you would probably go home in despair, retreat into your bed, pull the duvet over your head and push the world away. At that point in time, you may be too low to do the things you need to and you need a medication boost to get you onto the first rung of the ladder back to normality. But antidepressants are not the long-term solution.

Understanding exactly how antidepressants work and what your role is in helping them to work better and then coming off them will speed up the whole process and ensure they are the short-term boost they're intended to be.

I am not going to tell you to NOT take them and I'm certainly not going to tell you to stop taking antidepressants, you should **always consult your doctor**, but I am going to explain how you can help them work and how they should work in tandem with your own natural systems.

Modern Prozac based antidepressants are called SSRIs (selective serotonin re-uptake inhibitors), meaning they slow down the reabsorption rate of serotonin.

Serotonin is vitally important; we produce it naturally and we also reabsorb it.

You could say we produce our own fuel that use it up in the process of the day and so we need to keep producing it or it depletes to critical levels, aka 'depression.'

I explained in the previous chapter how serotonin floats across from one brain cell to another via the synaptic gap to make the connections between neurons and carry messages. The other side of that synaptic gap there are receptors. The more receptors you have, the quicker the serotonin is re-absorbed; SSRIs 'block' some of the receptors so that serotonin is kept hanging around in the synaptic gap a bit longer, making the positive connections between the brain cells stronger.

Serotonin is also your 'happy' chemical, you know that feeling of being on top of the world, you've got a bounce in your step, you just feel invincible, you can cope with anything life throws at you – that's when you've got high levels of serotonin – it feels fantastic.

But you have to produce it!

When you are depressed, your serotonin levels have dipped below an acceptable level and the SSRIs are prescribed to help lift that level of serotonin back into normal parameters. You are not taking serotonin, the antidepressants just slow down the reabsorption rate of your naturally produced serotonin.

Antidepressants usually take up to 14 days to start working, then you feel a bit better and more like doing something.

When you do something positive, you create serotonin in the process, then you feel a bit better so you feel like doing something else.

You go up a level and your antidepressants hold you there, so you feel better again, happier and move motivated, so you do something else, then your antidepressants hold you there, and so on until you reach a level where you have sufficient serotonin floating around for your intellect to work out what needs to change and you're brave enough to make new decisions, you can solve problems and slowly learn how to maintain and produce your own serotonin levels.

Now, if you've been on antidepressants for years and they don't seem to be doing you any good or you're afraid to come off them, it's because you haven't learned what you need to do to maintain good levels of serotonin yourself.

This is why you can't suddenly come off antidepressants, your serotonin levels would quickly plummet, you need to come off them slowly checking you are maintaining your own serotonin levels to an extent where the crutch provided by antidepressants are no longer needed.

Ultimately, in order to eliminate depression from your life, you need to learn how to create serotonin yourself.

This is something we all need to learn because natural serotonin is so much more powerful than any medication, chemical or drug you can take to simulate the effects.

# Chapter 15 – Chemical Consumption

I am not a dietician but my job here is to advise you on what you can do to help yourself out of depression, so I am going to touch on healthy eating for a moment because what you choose to consume will contribute to your chemical composition.

Your blood has the job of carrying nutrients, oxygen and antibodies around your body and it also removes things that shouldn't be there.

You need to be aware that whatever you are putting into your body in the way of consuming food, alcohol, nicotine and drugs or chemicals you're absorbing through your skin, will have an effect on your body, not least your moods – good and bad.

Sugars for example, and simple carbohydrates (bread, chips, pizza base, crisps, cakes, biscuits, pasta etc) that convert quickly in to sugar will give you an instant but momentary spike in blood sugar levels.

Your body can be quite lazy at producing serotonin if you've got out of the habit, so if it can't get the real deal, it will go for the quickest substitute it can persuade you to consume; sugars, alcohol, nicotine and drugs can all be serotonin substitutes.

It is very common for depression and weight gain to be present at the same time.

A symptom of depression is low motivation, so making an effort with food doesn't come easily or naturally. Reaching for fast foods or pre-prepared easy microwave or oven meals starts to become a habit.

But what often gets ignored are all the extra chemicals the food industry adds to the food to make it taste better, look better and last longer in the packaging.

All these extra chemicals are toxins. No, they're not going to kill you on their own in an instant, but your body doesn't know what to do with them, so it will either store them in fat cells or it just has to work extra hard at getting rid of them. Your body and blood, although amazing, can only do so much, so if they're spending all their time using energy and resources in eliminating toxins that you are doing to best to poison your body with, then is it any wonder you feel crap and have no energy?

In Chapter 3, Is Depression An Allergy, you learned about the recent research into inflammation caused by an allergic reaction being a contributing cause of depression. It stands to reason that your body could be reacting to the toxins and foods you're consuming that are alien to your blueprint.

You don't necessarily have to go out and buy organic everything, but do reduce the consumption of fast foods, ready-made sauces and meals and simple carbohydrates such as bread, pasta and sugar, and start introducing clean healthy foods.

Alcohol is a depressant – if you've got depression, don't drink it for now.

Nicotine is a stimulant

All drugs alter your chemical balance

You are a perfectly functioning, efficient machine that still operates under the extreme adverse conditions you put it under, is it any wonder it starts to break down when you don't look after it properly?

There are plenty of super healthy fast foods – eggs, they're fast food; it is quicker (and cheaper) to make an omelette than it is to order a takeaway. It's easier (and cheaper) to put a baked potato in the oven than a pizza (you've got to cut off packaging with a pizza). It just takes giving it some thought and changing habits.

It may take some research and re-education about what is healthy. It's a more positive and proactive pastime than watching TV.

The main point I'm making is that if you consume chemicals that are not naturally part of our diet and we're not designed to eat, they will affect your mood.

We take our bodies for granted; we consume poisonous chemicals on a daily basis that individually don't do any harm. But they're not on an individual basis any more, we consume greater and greater quantities of toxins every day that are having a detrimental affect, not only our body but our mind and emotions.

If you are determined to beat depression, this is an easy thing to adjust. You choose to consume them, you can choose not to as well.

# Chapter 16 - Caught in the Downpour

When you consider what you've learned so far about how modern life has deviated so drastically from our primitive blue print, it is any wonder that humans, amazing, but ultimately a fragile biological organism, have become caught in the middle of a combination of social conditions and dietary changes.

It confirms that it's not your fault you've become trapped in depression, but it is within your power to start making changes immediately to readdress the imbalance and distortion and, perhaps more importantly, it is your responsibility to make the choices that will rebalance your mind and body.

To summarise what we've learned so far:-

Your negative thought patterns are creating adrenaline that is suppressing any good serotonin or dopamine you might have. But because of the prolonged periods of withdrawal from activities and behaviours that create serotonin and dopamine, those levels have deplete to critical, making it difficult to do the very things you need to do to create them again.

It's a vicious cycle isn't it?

But what you can understand so far is that there are three things we're now going to focus on in order to rebalance your mind and body:-

1. Burning off adrenalin

2. Creating more serotonin and dopamine
3. Being aware of the unhealthy chemicals you're consuming, conscious of the direct effect your diet has on your mind and body and perhaps revisit what you believe is a 'healthy' diet.

Now it's time to start redressing the balance and get yourself back to the 'real' you.

# Chapter 17 – How to Rebalance Your Chemicals

It's important to accept that you are in control of your chemical balance and you can manipulate the levels yourself by your thoughts and behaviours. You're already doing it, just in the wrong way.

As you become more tuned to taking control of your thoughts and feelings, you will start to become more naturally aware of how your feelings relate to your neurotransmitter levels. Your body will want to keep them topped up, but quite often we ignore the signals because we don't understand what they mean.

This is something we learn more about in Part 3, Maintaining Happiness.

Serotonin gives very clear messages, when you know what to listen or look out for and then, of course, it is up to you to do something about it.

We often get things in the wrong order or misinterpret what our body is telling us. There is a huge difference between mental exhaustion due to lack of serotonin and physical exhaustion, but they can feel the same.

Feeling down, in a low mood or miserable and 'can't be bothered' are very clear signals that serotonin levels are low and you need to do something to top them up.

Physical exhaustion usually means you need to rest and replenish fuel supplies – food. Mental exhaustion is helped through increasing serotonin and dopamine levels or have a natural amount of sleep if you have been sleep deprived - doing nothing or sitting in front of the TV doesn't help at all.

It is worth noting at this stage that once you have your neurotransmitters balanced, which can take no time at all, you do need to keep them balanced, which takes constant practice. Just as you need to eat regularly because your food converts into energy that is used up and you have to refuel or eat again, neurotransmitters get used up in the same way. You create them, you use them and you need to replenish.

Getting to know yourself better and what works best for you is an interesting exercise of self-discovery.

Everyone needs a healthy balance of neurotransmitters. Your personality type and what you enjoy doing will guide you in the most effective solutions. (Eating and watching TV need to be tweaked – you can eat health food and watch TV programmes for personal growth and development, but forget eating pizza whilst watching the latest Netflix series back to back all weekend).

You can perhaps remember times when you felt at your best and reflect on what was happening in your life at that time for clues to what works for you.

Creating the right mix of neurotransmitters falls into three broad categories:-

## Positive Activity

Doing stuff! Positive activity covers a broad range and includes physical activity. To someone in the depths of depression positive activity might be something as simple as getting out of bed before three o'clock in the afternoon and getting dressed. What is considered to be positive activity will differ from one person to another. The qualifying criteria of positive activity is something which you feel pleased for having done; something which gives you a sense of achievement. So positive activity might mean passing an exam, learning something new, cleaning the house, doing the washing-up, taking part in your favourite hobby or achieving something you've been meaning to do; whatever it is, as long as you get a sense of achievement out of it you're creating serotonin.

The bigger the achievement you feel the more serotonin you create so although to some people it may seem very basic - getting out of bed, having a shower and getting dressed - to someone who has severe depression, that can be a huge achievement.

Physical exercise within the positive activity category is something which benefits everybody, and the powerful effect exercise has on the mind cannot be underestimated. It is a mistake to assume that exercise is about the effects on the body, although still good this is just a side-effect. The primary benefits are happening in your mind and in the creation of serotonin, dopamine and other positive hormones and chemicals such as endorphins one of the more commonly known hormones that make you feel good. Endorphins are also painkillers; your natural opioids, so also help you cope with pain.

Our primitive ancestors were built for an active lifestyle. Everything was labour intensive - hunting, gathering food, preparing a meal, building a shelter; every part of their daily lives included physical activity. So our blueprint is designed for physical activity which may have been the long-distance hunt, the nomadic moving around, or short bursts of energy with strength and muscle exercise - there's no doubt that, back then our lives were considerably more physically active than they are today.

Unfortunately however, as we have developed our big brains we have spent much time, energy and money inventing technologies that substitute the physical activity we were naturally designed for. Every effort now goes into convenience. We have many labour saving devices in our homes - we have dishwashers, washing machines and vacuum cleaners, microwaves, our bread is already made for us, as is butter and cheese - even as recently as 200 years ago, before the Industrial Revolution all these things would have been done by hand. However, time and progress have marched on resulting in the elimination from our lives of the very activities which kept us functioning at our most mentally and physically healthy.

The paradox of our intellect inventing all these labour saving devices is in the extra time we have to spend at our jobs working harder and neglecting the activities which keep us mentally healthy, so we can afford to buy the labour saving devices that are taking the place of mentally healthy activities.

Have you ever experienced catching your own fish or growing your own vegetables, cooking it and eating them – isn't that the best meal in the world? You know this sense of achievement.

Now of course we don't have to go out hunting and catch our own dinner and it would be idiotic to dispose of all our technology and I'm not suggesting you reject modern life.

But being aware that you are designed for physical activity and that your chemical balance that affects your moods and motivation is so tightly intertwined with physical activity will help you to learn how you can simulate and substitute essential physical activities into your daily life to reap the rewards of serotonin that you need.

There is also another beneficial function of exercise and that is to burn off adrenaline.

When you worry, or negatively forecast the future, the negativity is converted into anxiety. As anxiety levels rise, the amygdala is activated. This sends a message to the adrenal gland to release adrenaline into the bloodstream, enhancing the mind and body in preparation for the fight or flight. In short bursts when you're running away from hungry sabre tooth tigers this is very helpful indeed but your body cannot cope with a constant stream of adrenaline and it's exhausting. So you need to learn how to disperse it.

If your body and mind have been prepared for flight or fight then the best thing you can do is just that, run or fight. Of course I'm not suggesting you start a brawl in your street and you don't have to run a marathon when you get home every evening from work, but simulating the physical activity will burn off that adrenaline, energise your body and calm the mind.

## Positive Interaction

Being with other people is essential for our mental-health and fundamental in the survival of the human race.

Our modern lifestyles and technology have made it too easy for us to isolate ourselves and although it can be very therapeutic to get some space, privacy and time out from other people, modern society has enabled this to the extreme, which is having a negative impact on mental health.

Human beings are essentially pack animals, our strength and survival depends on working as part of a tribe. We don't have many natural defences, we're not poisonous, we don't taste nasty, we don't have spiky things all over our body and we can't run very fast so we need the physical and intellectual strength of the pack to survive and evolve. In primitive times, isolating yourself from your tribe would have meant certain death; so primitive man and woman received rewards for learning how to communicate well within their tribe. Everyone would have had a defined role, they would know their place and where they fitted in. Those rewards for communicating and cooperating with others successfully were feel-good neurotransmitters serotonin and dopamine and, as we already know, these neurotransmitters are essential to mental health.

Have you had the experience of saying 'yes' to an invitation from friends or relatives but as the evening draws nearer all you really want to do is flop in front of the TV with a glass of wine (same as you did the night before)? However, you can't think of a good enough excuse to get out of the engagement so you muster some energy and go anyway. You arrive thinking you'll stay an hour or so then make an excuse to leave. However, after an hour you have completely forgotten about your plans to go, you've found your second wind and you're thoroughly enjoying yourself. It doesn't take long to raise neurotransmitter levels sufficiently to feel the rewards from positive interaction.

When people live in social groups, families, communities, and tribes, if individuals fall on hard times become ill or need support, everyone pitches in to help and everyone is very aware of the other people within their community and their need. This is particularly important for mental health; people living in close-knit communities and families have that constant support whether they like it or not and if somebody is struggling emotionally, if they are worrying or feeling miserable, someone is always on hand to step in before it becomes a problem.

In our modern societies where it is so easy to isolate ourselves, these problems can rapidly decline beyond the control of the individual without being detected by anyone else.

If your life circumstances or choices have found you isolated from others, you don't have to suddenly seek out a commune to join, but it is important to understand the physiological need for other people in our lives, to have a role and understand where we fit in. You need to reconnect with people in person and make an effort to put yourself in social situations.

## Positive Thinking

I would like you to be mindful of three things about thinking

1. You are thinking all the time
2. Your brain is the control centre for your whole body

### 3. You are listening to you.

I have already delved into the side effects of negative thinking in depth and the importance of awareness of how we are thinking in earlier chapters, so lets now have a look at positive thinking and the benefits of practicing thinking in a positive way.

I'm sure that you will agree that decisions and actions are first made in your mind. You think, next you decide to do something and then you act and do it, or not as the case may be.

Many actions happen from the subconscious brain, driving is a good example of this. When you first learn to drive it's very complex - you have to think 'mirror, signal, gear, clutch, brake, accelerator' and you have to do it all at once and you might have thought to yourself 'how am I ever going to get all this?' But now you don't even think about it when you get in the car - it happens automatically.

Your brain at a subconscious level controls all breathing, your body temperature, your heart rate, fighting infection and digestion.

Of course it is necessary for some things to happen automatically without you consciously thinking about it, we would all go insane if we had to think about pumping blood around our body and breathing and, quite honestly, many of the functions our bodies perform are far too complicated for our simple conscious brain.

But you can accept that the brain is the control centre for your whole body. You are the driver and you are in charge.

How you use your imagination plays an important role in operating your control centre and how you direct it will affect your physical and emotional reactions.

You can experiment with it right now by bringing to mind an image of yourself doing something fun and exciting that you really enjoy which makes you happy. Take yourself back to a place or a time that was happy for you, a holiday perhaps, childhood memories, a night out with friends, the birth of a child (just examples, pick your own that means something to you).

Imagine how you feel, make it as real as you can, close your eyes and fill in as many details as you can with your imagination.

Now how do you feel?

Perhaps you have a smile on your face.

Imagining something good will create serotonin, the same as doing it. Your brain doesn't know the difference between imagination and reality, so when you imagine something positive for you, serotonin is created just as if you were really there.

Now imagine something you really like to eat, something that makes your mouth water, smell it, taste it, savor it..

Is your mouth watering?

That's a physical reaction just from using your imagination and it happens almost instantly – yes?

You can understand how powerful your thoughts are on your mind and body so everything you think –

EVERYTHING you think will have either a negative or positive impact on your physical and physiological systems.

I don't want you to do this right now, but when you think about something that did upset you or would upset you if it happened, it brings on powerful emotions.

You can sit here now and practice thinking about something happy, something mouthwatering and something upsetting and you can observe the effect it has on you physically and emotionally.

How powerful is that?

Let's bring it back to reality...

> you are doing this 'imagination' thinking every minute you are awake and what you are thinking about when you are awake is replaying when you are in REM sleep.

If you are thinking in a negative way all the time, which is the common thinking habit every depressed person has, can you see how this affects you emotionally and physically?

This is the baseline of what needs to change.

People who don't suffer from depression or anxiety do not think in a negative way by default, they generally live in the moment and think in terms of solutions when problems arise or difficult life events happen.

Everyone can feel miserable or think negatively at times, but people who don't suffer from depression quickly bounce back to their positive default, people with depression stay their and apply the negative thinking to all aspects of their life.

You can change your default setting, it's your brain, it's just going to take a bit of practice, until you have a new habit.

# Chapter 18 – Why Practice?

Practicing something is how you programme your mind. You don't have a keyboard or mouse to input information, so how you think and what you do is your input mechanism.

Over time what you do and think forms neural networks in your brain and becomes embedded in your subconscious. When this happens what you have been practicing becomes automatic - you don't have to consciously think about it, you just do it.

Reading and writing are good examples, you had to learn, but now you just 'do'. Riding a bicycle is another one, I'm sure you've heard the saying 'you never forget how to ride a bike'.

There are literally thousands of actions we perform daily that, at one time, we had to learn and practice but now we just do, subconsciously.

Think of 'how you think' as a practice that you have been doing since a baby. If you have practiced thinking negatively you will have formed those neural networks in your brain and will do it subconsciously.

However, you can change it and start practicing thinking in a positive beneficial way the moment you choose to.

This analogy that explains how this work very well:

*Imagine you need to cross a field every day from your front door to your car. You come out of your front door and go through the gate into the field and you follow the path across the field. You've been doing this for years and there is a well worn path that you don't even think about taking, you just follow it because it's the path you always follow. It's not a particularly easy path, you often hurt yourself tripping over obstacles, but it's the path that you automatically use anyway.*

*One day, perhaps after a particularly bad fall or you realise other people seem to cross the field easily and you look up and you see the path for what it is and you realise that it isn't the best or easiest route across the field. The problem is that it's the only clear path available at the moment. If you want to take a different route you have to make a new path. But you are so fed up with following a path that you get hurt using, you make up your mind to find a different way.*

*So the next day, you go up to the gate in the field and you look for a new route and you discover a much easier way across the field, it takes you through beautiful clearings with flowers and birds and you feel truly happy when you're walking along this path. You don't have to look down at the hazards, you can look up at all the beauty around you instead.*

*The next day, you take the new path again and it gets easier, you remember the route you found the day before. This time you're a little more confident in your new path, it's not unknown now so you're not afraid of where it might take you, so you enjoy the journey. You resolve to keep following this new path.*

*A few days later you have something on your mind as you go out of your house and you forget the new path, instead you automatically return to the habit of your old path without thinking. But you soon become aware that you're off down the wrong path, so you stop and cross over to the new path again*

*This happens a few more times, but the more you practice and the more frequently you consciously take the new path, the more natural it becomes.*

*As you practice walking on the new path something else happens, you start to wear away the grass on your new route making an actual path and the grass gets an opportunity to grow over the old path so that path fades away.*

*It's not too long before you go out of your house in the morning and you take the new happy path automatically because it's the path you just take every day, you don't think about it, you just do it because that's what you do. There is now an established path there and the old path has completely grown over and faded away.*

This is exactly what is happening in your brain when you practice new positive habits, you are creating new positive neural pathways and the old negative ones are fading away because you don't have any need for them any more.

Initially it might be a frustrating process of constantly correcting yourself because your brain has been trained to do something different and can slip back to the old default habits. But, if you want to lift yourself out of depression and you want to change your default enough, you can and you will do it.

It is just like practicing any new skill - you have to do it regularly and consistently - practice!

How do you think the top sports people in the world became that good at it? Practice.

Do you think they found it easy every day? I doubt it.

Do you think they made mistakes and got it wrong at times? Probably.

Did they give up? No.

Learning to be aware of how are you thinking and turning it into true positive thinking is a skill that will empower you to do anything you set your mind to.

There's another great secret and benefit to positive thinking and that is whatever you set your mind to focus on is the direction in which you go.

In Part 3 I will let you in on the secrets of how the mind works and the science behind the Law of Attraction. You will learn to manipulate your world into anything you want it to be.

But that's a step away, let's master the basics first and set the foundations so you can build a solid future

.

# Chapter 19 – Step by Step

Remember what I said about serotonin? When you have depression, your serotonin levels are very low and you need to build them up. Serotonin is going to help you form those new positive neural networks in your mind.

You do this by practicing

> **Positive Activity**
>
> **Positive Thinking**
>
> **Positive Interaction**

But you're going to do this one step at a time.

Serotonin helps you cope with anything, it motivates you (gives you energy), it makes you braver, it helps you cope with physical fear, it boosts your immune system and helps you cope with pain.

When you are starting with very low levels however, the smallest of things can feel overwhelming, getting motivated is a struggle and your default is negative thinking and believing you can't do it. You can, but your own subconscious negative belief is sabotaging your conscious desire to do it.

You can overcome this and I'm going to show you how. This bit is very important.

You're going to start practicing a combination of all three of the positive things you need to do, but you're going to start in a very small way with the one that comes easiest to you.

You will set yourself **small** goals that you're going to achieve, It doesn't matter how small they are or what they are as long as they are achievable to you. The mistake people make is to decide they're going to get up at six o'clock in the morning and go to the gym for the first time in five years. – this is too big and when you don't do it, you will beat yourself up, feel even worse and keep yourself locked in depression. You cannot leap out of depression, you have to climb out slowly, one step at a time

This explains why, when people tell you to 'snap out of it' you can't.

You need to create and build up serotonin, that's what is going to motivate you to do the bigger things, eventually, but start at a level that is right for you. Then when you achieve that small goal you set – BE PLEASED WITH YOURSELF.

Give yourself a big pat on the back and smile from ear to ear!

No one is there to judge you; this is about you being pleased for yourself **without scolding yourself for not doing more** and getting that serotonin reward. This is YOUR journey, not someone else's, there is no benchmark of what you should achieve. You set the benchmark and when you hit it you reward yourself.

Let go of negative thoughts and feelings about not doing what you think you 'should' do – we do not live in 'Should-land'

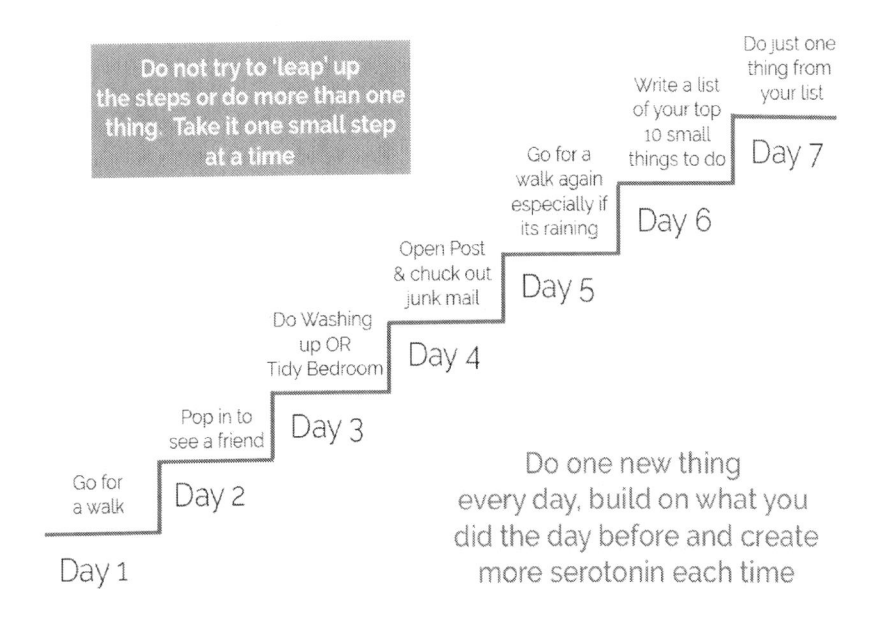

```
                                                              Do just one
                                                              thing from
                                              Write a list    your list
Do not try to 'leap' up                       of your top
the steps or do more than one                 10 small
thing. Take it one small step     Go for a    things to do   Day 7
at a time                         walk again
                                  especially if
                                  its raining   Day 6
                        Open Post
                        & chuck out
                        junk mail   Day 5
              Do Washing
              up OR
              Tidy Bedroom  Day 4
     Pop in to
     see a friend  Day 3
Go for                        Do one new thing
a walk   Day 2                every day, build on what you
                              did the day before and create
Day 1                         more serotonin each time
```

The details are not a guide of what you should do, they are just examples. The important things to notice are

- Do small things
- Do something extra every day you haven't been doing
- Take one step at a time and keep stepping.

It might be day six or week six before you're even up to making a list of things you need to do, but as long as you're moving forwards a little bit every day you are going in the right direction

Building serotonin takes time to start with, but you will notice that, if you do something every day, the things you do will become bigger things and you will do them without thinking and without that internal battle.

At some point you need to get disciplined and override that primitive brain that will come up with all the arguments NOT to do what you have set your intention to do.

Leave the big decisions and big actions until later, just put them down and forget them for now. The purpose of building up your serotonin levels, apart from motivation, energy and coping with day to day life, is to strengthen the connections in your intellectual brain. It is your intellect that will work out the answers you're looking for and come up with solutions to your problems, the best thing you can do is get out of its way.

Your job is to create serotonin so your intellect can start functioning at its best. When you're ready it WILL tell you what you need to do about the big things, trust it.

Think of it like a car engine - if you don't have oil in the engine, the engine will dry up and can't function. You need to put the oil back in so it runs smoothly again. (Luckily you don't overheat and blow up without serotonin, you get depressed, have no energy or motivation and life gets difficult.)

# Chapter 20 – How to Practice Positive Thinking

Positive thinking is vital for creating new neural pathways as we've learnt and I'm sure you've heard people say "think positively", but the question usually left unanswered is 'how?'

We've looked in some depth about what negative thinking covers, however, it's largely left as an assumption that everyone knows how to think positively. But if you've had a lifetime of thinking negatively or perhaps not had any awareness before of how you are thinking, you may well not know how to think in a positive way.

This is similar to a parent saying to a teenager 'I will treat you like an adult when you act like one', but how is a teenager supposed to know how to act like an adult?

It's a learning process that happens with trial, error and practice, exactly the same as any learning process and this is also true of positive thinking.

Remember the analogy of a teenager when you are getting frustrated if you lapse into negative thinking or you don't get it immediately – it's takes at least seven years of practice, trial and many errors before a teenager learns how to be an adult and in some cases many more years!

Relax and accept that you are about to learn a new discipline that will change your life for the better.

To help you learn how to think in a positive way, the following are a number of exercises that you can practice which will help retain your brain and form the positive neural pathways.

## Exercise 3 – Self Recognition

Write everything down that you can and you DO do on a daily basis. Track your day writing all the things you do no matter how small or insignificant you think it is.

I had an email from a lady recently who said to me "you don't understand how hard it is, I can't do any more than look after my two boys."

I pointed out to her that looking after two young children (especially boys with bags of energy) is a big deal; she IS doing that. Think of everything that goes into looking after two children on your own – in my opinion that's massive. She was just focusing on what she believed she could not do and that was causing the anxiety that kept her in her primitive brain.

If you are working – well give yourself a pat on the back; despite having depression, you are still going to work.

If you are looking after your sick mother – give yourself a pat on the back; despite having depression, you are caring for someone else.

Switch your focus from what you can't do or not doing to what you are doing and give yourself credit.

Make that list now.

## Exercise 4 – Reprioritise Your Life

You will do what you have to do.

Going back to the lady who could not do any more than look after her two boys.

Her boys were clearly a priority in her life; if one of her boys was sick or needed something for school – I think she would be able to rise to that challenge.

When I had depression, I walked my dog for an hour in the morning and the evening every day come wind, rain or shine and in the dark – because it was a priority for me, it was something I believed I HAD to do, I had no choice (my dog wouldn't let me get away with not going). The consequences of not doing that was nothing but an annoying dog really, but to me it was a top priority that couldn't be missed, so I did it even though I couldn't be bothered to wash my hair.

So look at what you can and are doing –

1. **Make a list of the priorities in your life.**
    a. What is so important to you that you will do it, no matter what?
    b. Where do you get the energy from to do that?
    c. Why are you motivated to do those things?

You have a choice in everything you do, it is you who is putting the priority and importance value on that activity and you can redefine your priorities over other things.

The two most common excuses I hear are:-

- I don't have time
- I can't afford it

Both of these things are about priorities and nothing else. You will find the time to do the things you HAVE to and you will find the money to pay for the things you HAVE to. Who is deciding the 'HAVE to'? - You are.

2. **You don't have to reveal this to anyone else, but it is vital that you are honest with yourself.**
   a. How much time do you spend in front of the TV?
   b. Could you get up 30 minutes earlier?
   c. If you HAD to, where would you find extra time?
   d. How much do you spend on convenience food, bottles of wine or beer, going out, things you don't really need?

Now give yourself a number from 0 to 10 for how important curing yourself from depression is?

Is curing yourself of depression a higher priority than watching TV?

The truth and mean it.

## Exercise 5 – Energize Yourself

Do something right now – I don't care how silly you feel, if you're listening to this in audio format, listen to the instructions, pause, do this exercise and then resume the audio.

Go into a room on your own – get some privacy.

Put an upbeat piece of music on the you like

And DANCE to it.

Jump around, force a smile on your face and dance until it has finished, feeling positive about it.

Then after you've finished, notice how do you feel? (Apart from silly!)

How did you just get the energy to dance?

Right in that moment you made it a priority and you did it, without thinking, you just did.

Draw on this knowledge to do other small things.

For the next 11 days – do a dance a day

## Exercise 6 - Daily Check In

This is something I do every day, it keeps me grounded and grateful for what I do have in life.

Start practicing this every day and form a new habit, when you look back in three months time, you will be amazed at how far you've come if you keep up the positive practices and keep taking those steps.

Get a plain lined paper book or pad of paper – you're going to write these things in it every day.

1. **What am I most grateful for in my life today?**

   Write five things, it can be having good friends, a roof over your head, a family that loves you, it can be materialistic things, it can be inner resources you have, things you've learnt – it's up to you, if you can think of more than five, then write them down, but do this every day.

2. **Today my dominant feeling is….**

   You're going to decide how you want to feel – and make it a positive thing! Whatever you like, motivated, inspired, calm, grateful, happy, creative, organised.

   How you think determines how you feel and how you feel will determine how you behave, so think and decide how you're going to feel, don't examine your feelings, decide you're fed up and go with it for the day – it is your decision.

### 3. My intention today is ....

This is where you set yourself a small goal or something you want to do, achieve, start, finish or just something positive you're going to be for the day.

For example,

My intention today is to be easy-going around the children.

My intention today is to cook a healthy dinner for the family.

My intention by the end of the day is to have started ....

My intention today is to go out of the house and have a coffee in town.

### 4. Throw it to the universe

This is something that is on your mind that you can't do anything about right now - throw it to the universe to deal with. Move responsibility for worrying about or dealing with something you can't change right now from you to the universe.

Universe, please come up with a solution for my job situation

Universe, please look after my sister's health

Universe, please give me ideas for how I can come up with the funds to ....

### 5. Wild Hair Intention

Your wild hair intention is something big and crazy. It's your dream, what you want to have or have happen in the future, it can be anything you want it to be, just make it big and outrageous and something that would make you ultimately happy if you had it or achieved it.

With all the points above, make sure you give your subconscious <u>positive</u> instruction. Your mind can't act on what you don't want, it can only act on what you do want. So, for example, don't write, 'My intention today is to NOT sit in front of the TV all day'. Your brain doesn't know what to do with that. Turn the statement into something positive like 'My intention today is to go into town and have a coffee' or 'my intention today is to go for a 30 minute walk'.

## Exercise 7 – Mind Distraction Technique

You are thinking too much – fact.

When your mind is idle or not actively occupied in something positive, it defaults to ruminating on problems and worries, which are all negative.

Remember those negative neural pathways you've formed. Well, when you're not actively doing something you have to concentrate on, until you've allowed those networks to fade away, which will happen over time, you will subconsciously fall back into old thinking habits.

An easy way of keeping yourself out of that trap is to have something else to focus on.

I understand that motivation is difficult initially so you need to find something that doesn't take much effort and my top suggestion for this is:-

## Audio books

Anytime you are doing something manual that you don't have to think about – driving, cleaning, ironing, cooking, lying in bed at night before going to sleep or anything else you do that involves physical rather than mental action, listen to an audio book.

This is not the same as listening to the radio or music which you can do subconsciously. You have to follow a story, you need to use your conscious mind to do that and while it is, it cannot think about the negatives at the same time. The longer you're out of the negative primitive brain, the quicker the negative connections will drop and fade away.

I taught myself to like ironing, would you believe - with audio books! I hated ironing with a passion, but found myself in a role where I had to do it. The mere thought of having to do the ironing made me stroppy, but I had discovered audio books a while ago and the whole exercise turned around into something I enjoyed doing because I had an excuse to listen to a really good book. Reading is something I hardly every do, unless it's research, but I do enjoy a good book. Audio books catch the attention of your conscious mind and your imagination.

Many clients have given me feedback about the positive effect they have also experienced listening to audio books.

If you like a good book, then great, get a novel, but also hugely beneficial are self help books, positive psychology, positive affirmation type books, they will all help to retrain your brain.

## Exercise 8 – Self Development

The most valuable investment you can make is in yourself.

If you have problems or issues to overcome that seem so big you will never be able to, the way to overcome them is to grow yourself to be bigger than the problem.

Invest in yourself and in your continual self-improvement. Your brain will love it. You have billions of brain cells; they need to be filled with stuff.

Right now you're filling them with negative self-harming, self-sabotaging stuff made up in your imagination. Stop that and fill them with positive information that is going to grow you, make you bigger and better than your problems and take you to a new level of wisdom.

You can find your own sources of interest and you might even want to learn a new skill, but if you want some pointers, the people I follow regularly and read/listen to are;-

- Tony Robbins
- Zig Ziglar
- Stephen Covey
- Jim Rohn
- Prof Stephen Peters
- John C Maxwell

# Chapter 21 – Relapse Rate

Whilst depression is successfully and easily cured, it does have a notoriously high relapse rate. These are the reasons why:-

The person is relying on medication to make them feel better and when they do, they start finding solutions to the problems and the problems go away and they feel better again, life is back to normal.

But they never understand properly what has happened neurologically and practically. They don't learn what needs to change and that it's internal changes, their thought patterns and how they deal with situations, not the situation itself. Humans are by nature habitual, we follow the same patterns of behaviour again and again, but that doesn't mean we have to. It is our brain, our mind and our habits, we can change any part of it we want to.

There is a lot of ignorance and arrogance displayed by the person who says "that just how I am" - the ignorance of not knowing there is a choice to be different and the arrogance of thinking no change is necessary – everyone else can just deal with it.

Learning what needs to change from within and practicing doing things differently can prevent relapses.

However, another reason relapses happen is because along the way neural pathways have been formed in the brain for the depressive thoughts and behaviours. Although these pathways fade away with time when they're not used, if someone who is prone to depression lets the primitive part of the brain take control from time to time, those negative neural pathways will re-engage. The good news however is that when you have learned how to bring yourself out of depression the first time, you can do it any time you want and get quicker at it. It's not long before you notice little warning signs that your primitive brain is taking control and you will develop 'go to' quick fixes that can and will snap you out of it.

You can become self aware of what you need to be doing to maintain a healthy mental state and notice quickly when the balance is starting to wobble.

It takes practice and it's a practice we all need to do – the people who don't have depression practice regularly naturally. Think of it like this:-

There is a neglected run down house, for years it's not been maintained properly, it's just been patched up here and there using the wrong materials. No one has taken responsibility for this house, as they walk past looking at its sorry state, they might think, it's the weather, the rain, the wind beating it down, vandals, kids using it as a hideout, tramps sleeping rough ... and they might think the materials were defective because all the houses around it look OK. They might even think the local council should do something about it, no one wants to live near a house like that, some one else should take responsibility for it – whose fault it is anyway?

It's not the house that's defective, it's how it's been taken care of.

You are that house and you have a choice, you can choose to patch it up again with medication and then just leave it and hope for the best, until you need to redo the same job in two years time: Or you can start maintaining it.

If you choose to, you can rebuild it into the finest house on the street. You're going to do it! You can get advice on the right materials to use, the techniques and know how, but you are going to do it and when it is the best it can be, you're going to learn how to maintain it so it never falls into disrepair again.

1. The first step is to decide you're going to do it.
2. The second step is to take responsibility for doing it.
3. The third step is don't give up on it.

Even if you don't know the whole journey yet, just keep putting one foot in front of the other, one step at a time, until you get there. And you will get there, you just need to start the journey and not give up.

It's not always going to be easy – but nothing worth having in life is, that's the reward, and the harder it seems, the bigger reward at the end when you know you've done it and you've done it by yourself.

## You can do it.

Taking responsibility for doing something and taking action is the key.

No one can blame you for the depression because no one ever explains these things to us or tells you what to do to prevent depression. It creeps up on us and before we realise, we're unable to function, unable to focus and we crawl back into bed and pull the duvet over our head.

But you can put it right by changing how you think about things and readdressing the chemical balance in your mind and body by doing the positive things in life that will create serotonin and dopamine. It's up to you.

# Part 3

# Living on Cloud 9

# Maintaining Happiness

# Chapter 22 – Living On Cloud 9

What does "Living on Cloud 9" mean?

I googled it and found

## 'a state of perfect happiness'

or the one I like in particular is

***"I'm on cloud nine" is an expression used when someone is extremely happy. Not a care in the world. Everything is going your way. You feel carefree as if floating on a cloud.***

Yep, that resonates with me and I could go a step further.

When I think about being on Cloud 9 an image pops into my head: it's one of those days that I'm just inexplicably happy, nothing in particular has happened to 'make' me happy, I just feel so happy I could burst and I can't do anything about the smile that's fixed on my face. I'm walking along with a spring in my step, full of energy, my head is up, I notice the birds, flowers and other people around me. I am completely in the moment. I make eye contact with people in the street and I smile at them – they smile back, my happiness is contagious.

**That's how it feels – doesn't it sounds wonderful? It is.**

On a practical level, the secret to 'Living on Cloud 9' is keeping yourself topped up to overflowing with serotonin, making sure you burn off any adrenaline you might create and being vigilant of how you are thinking, so you can stop any negative thoughts in their tracks and do something that creates positive ones.

When you have everything balanced and learn how to maintain it, you will be operating from your intellectual brain consistently. This is your responsibility and it's in your interest to do so because when your intellect is engaged and functioning efficiently, life is easy, you're happy, opportunity and Lady Luck pop in for breakfast and everything is hunky dory.

Of course life still happens and shit happens, there is a lot we're not in control of, but on Cloud 9 we can decide the shit doesn't smell so bad after all. Or to be less basic about it and to use a well worn cliché – life sometimes gives us lemons; on Cloud 9 we love making lemonade.

Problems become opportunities, we're attractive to other people, we become a magnet attracting lots of new people into our lives, we're fit and healthy, our social life is buoyant, we have passions and interests in life and nothing is too much trouble.

Life is exactly how you want it to be on Cloud 9 and how it is, is how you want it to be.

Is this how you would choose to go through life if you could?

Well, you can, it is a choice.

If you've just dismissed that statement and you don't believe it, then you haven't learned the secrets to making yourself happy yet - you need to go back to Part 2, follow the exercises and practice.

You cannot leap onto Cloud 9 and expect to understand the secrets of how to live there permanently. You need to learn how to get there first, step by step.

This is the mistake people are making and why the relapse rate for depression is so high. They are not learning (or accepting) the truth behind why they are depressed and how to get themselves out; it either just happens or the medication helps. Temporarily they can feel great, but are not in control of their happiness and, just as a cloud doesn't have a solid base, if they haven't built their own solid happiness base, they will slowly sink back to the black cloud of depression.

## Chapter 23 – The Secret

*Imagine you have learned to walk on a tightrope and you are pleased with your efforts to do it proficiently. When you are practicing your tightrope walking, you love it, everyone else is impressed with you as well – happy days!*

*But conditions are not always perfect for tightrope walking and the more experienced and confident you become, the more challenging the conditions you encounter. Some days it is blowing a gale, other days people are throwing things at you, or rain makes the rope slippery, but you know it hurts when you fall off, so despite the adverse conditions all around, you are determined to stay balanced.*

You can use your own analogy, but the secret to staying put on Cloud 9 is practice and learning how to stay balanced so that, if something comes along to wobble your cloud, you're not going to fall off, you steady the cloud instead.

Once you are out of depression staying in your intellectual brain is about learning how to recognise your own unique signs that you're wobbling and doing something – taking the action that is right for you to bounce back.

The relapse rate for depression is notoriously high because people don't learn this bit. They come out of depression without ever understanding the truth behind depression or learning what part they played in the depression or the recovery, and they go back to the same life and habits they had before without making the internal changes, shifting their mindset or making practical changes in their life.

Everything is OK for a while, but the next time 'life' happens, they relapse and follow the same cycles of behaviour.

So if you would prefer to live a happy life on Cloud 9 and you want to stay there you need to do three things:-

1. Take responsibility for yourself and your happiness
2. Become self aware
3. Take action when you wobble

Tuning in to your intuition and becoming aware of your unique 'signs' is the fine tuning you can learn when you thoroughly understand how to come out of depression.

## What are your signs?

To recognise your signs, we need to quickly revisit some of the characteristics of the primitive brain:

### Negative thinking:-

- Negative forecasting of the future
- Negative introspecting about life, yourself and the past
- Obsessive thoughts and behaviours
- Resenting other people
- Worrying about what other people think.
- Unwanted habits, alcohol, smoking, drugs, gambling

- Unhealthy eating patterns, especially starches and sugars

## Physical symptoms:-

- Insomnia or sleeping disorders
- Exhaustion and Apathy
- Upset stomach or butterflies
- Other physical symptoms and illnesses
- Contracting colds and flu more than usual.
- Headaches

I can't tell you exactly what will happen for you as everyone is unique in the symptoms they develop, but the earlier you can jump in and rebalance, the quicker and easier you can hop back onto your happy cloud. Don't wait to be feeling miserable, as you tune into your intuition and become self aware, you will notice more tangible things happening that warn you when your serotonin levels have dropped.

I have been practicing keeping myself balanced for years now and I teach these techniques to help others. So I think I'm pretty good at staying on my Cloud 9, engineering my life the way I want it to be. But I am also human and I have to practice exactly the same as everyone else does or suffer the consequences!

From time to time I can slide if I am not paying attention and I don't do the things that I know keep my serotonin and dopamine levels high.

My early warning signs are these:-

- **Cheese sandwiches.**

Yes, cheese sandwiches, bizarre, I know! This is such a strong signal for me that even my close friends and family will know that if they see me eating cheese sandwiches, I'm struggling emotionally. Bread is a simple carbohydrate that is quickly turned into sugar (serotonin substitute) and for me this becomes a binge habit leading to a lot of weight gain if I allow it to continue unchecked. Cheese sandwiches I love and it's a childhood thing, but that is irrelevant to my life today. It is a warning sign that I need to do something to top up serotonin levels immediately because they are already too low.

When I'm in a good place, I have a very healthy diet, but when I'm not, my diet and subsequently my health, confidence and self esteem suffer.

- **I start thinking about ex-partners.**

This is introspecting about the past. It could be anything for someone else, mine is just an example I'm prepared to share so that others can identify their warning signs. In my mind I either focus on the fondness we shared instead of the reasons we split up or I revisit old resentments. Neither are useful in any way whatsoever, they are just a waste of brain energy and space, but they are a sign for me that I need to make changes.

When I'm in a good place, I don't even think about past relationships.

- **I get Migraines**

Migraines have been attributed to low serotonin levels and it is certainly the case for me. When my life goes off balance, I get cluster migraines – a very physical sign that I need to do something to pull it back immediately.

Physical symptoms are often a sign that you have let it go too far and your primitive mind has stepped in and is actively causing conditions to physically stop you doing whatever it is that is leading to the anxiety.

Learn to tune in to your early warning signs, write a list of what you think they might be.

# Chapter 24 - Mindfulness

Evidence is growing for the positive effects on your mental health that Mindfulness has.

Mindfulness is a combination of meditation and some basic principles that provide you with tools for coping with life.

## Principles of Mindfulness

### Awareness

We must first notice what is present before we can become comfortable with it. Although with hypnotherapy we focus on positive thinking, reducing the damaging effects of negative thinking, it can be counterproductive to keep 'pushing out' the negative thoughts and feelings. The harder you push out, the stronger they will push back, after all it's your primitive brain trying to warn you about dangers. So learning to be consciously aware of your internal thoughts and acknowledging that these things are happening without getting involved, recognising that they're coming from your imagination, is the first principle.

### Present-moment focus

The mind can focus in so many directions: past, present, future, abstract notions or analytical problem solving, to name a few. All forms of thought have a useful role. In this practice, however, we prioritise awareness of the present moment. We are cultivating the ability to tune into sights, sounds, physical sensations, thoughts and emotions that are occurring in the present moment.

## Acceptance

Once we are aware of what we are experiencing, we can learn to accept it. That does not mean that we like it or that there isn't a better way for things to be; it just means that we are acknowledging the present reality without fighting it or trying to change it. Learning to accept other people around you for who they are without judgment, and accepting situations you cannot control or change or do anything about right now, is equally as important.

## Non-judgment

It is a common reaction for the mind to categorise experiences as good or bad, right or wrong, like it, don't like it. However, it is also possible to simply observe and describe sensations, thoughts or feelings without evaluating them. The mindset we will cultivate during meditation practice is that of curious interest and attentive observation rather than evaluation or judgment.

## Validation

Whatever you experience internally is valid—it is there for a reason, whether you understand it or not. It is not always necessary to understand the origins of an experience or a reaction in order to come to terms with it. Throughout meditation practice, as we notice thoughts, emotions, or physical sensations, we assume that our reactions are valid based on our learning history, our culture, or personality, etc. As such, we cultivate an attitude of validation.

## Tolerance

When you choose to tune in, you may find that some internal experiences are unpleasant or even painful. Rather than trying to immediately change them or block them out, we allow ourselves to experience the sensations, thereby cultivating tolerance for things that are uncomfortable.

## Compassion

Just as you would have compassion for a friend who is in pain, when you notice your own suffering, this creates an opportunity to cultivate compassion towards yourself. This concept is initially quite foreign to people who have developed a habit of self-criticism or self pity, but it can be powerfully healing when one learns to breathe fully into an attitude of self-compassion.

## Invitation

At times we notice that an old habit or reaction is not serving us well and could be worth revising. Perhaps the mind is festering in anger or the body is holding on to tension. Rather than chastising ourselves to let go and change, we gently invite openness to new possibilities.

## Patience

The process of growth and discovery can seem painstakingly slow at times. Therefore, we cultivate an attitude of patience toward our own process, because we all know that change is not easy.

## Practice

Understanding the above concepts can be inspiring, however, until these notions are put into practice, it's merely an entertaining intellectual exercise. Seeds that are not planted do not grow. Therefore, we make a commitment to actively practice exercises to reinforce these principles and cultivate our peace of mind and body.

## Mindful Meditation

Meditation and hypnosis, although having opposite beneficial effects, when used together are super effective.

They both work at a subconscious level but in different ways.

> Hypnosis helps build positive neural networks and make new connections in your intellectual.

> Mindful meditation helps you let go of unhelpful connections that you have inadvertently built.

Using both is an excellent daily maintenance routine for your mind.

You need to find your own rhythm within your daily routines, but I would suggest 20 minutes of mindful meditation in the morning when you get up, before you start your day, and listening to a hypnosis track when you are in bed ready to go to sleep at night.

I have included a link to a guided mindful meditation track (see Addendum 2). When you have learned the principles of meditation, you don't need to use the track, but you might find it helpful in the beginning.

Meditation is a practice and it is something you do need to practice. Don't worry if you find it difficult to relax your mind enough so it doesn't wander off initially, that's one of the things the guided meditation track will help you with and it is very normal for these things to happen. Just keep practicing.

## Mindful Meditation Practice

You can find a guided Mindful Meditation track at the following website address:

https://soundcloud.com/old-town-hypnotherapy/guided-mindful-meditation

Practice for 20 minutes every morning.

# Chapter 25 – Change

If you have depression or anxiety, something in your life needs to change and it might not be what you think it is.

Your intellect will know what it is – your intellect will come up with answers based on a proper assessment of the situation and is generally very positive.

Your primitive brain will focus on the problems and what you tend to think you need to change, but it isn't necessarily correct; let me give you some examples from past clients:-

I had a young lady come to see me for help with an eating disorder; she was bulimic. She was only 22 years old, but she was a professional horseracing jockey, so there was pressure to keep her weight down. All was going well and she was gradually starting to get herself a life back and gain confidence. One day she came for her appointment and announced that she had made a decision. She was happy and excited and I asked her what it was – "I'm going to Australia" she announced.

"Wow" I said, "that's a bit of a curve ball, where has that come from?"

She explained that she had worked out that it was horses and horseracing she loved and there were other forms of horseracing all around the world where she could earn a good living, but what she was doing at the moment wasn't the right type of racing for her, she just thought it was the only option before. She bought me in a newspaper clipping about her winning her last UK race and opening up to the press about her struggle with bulimia (which incidentally had faded away).

That was a big life change, but another client I had just made a small tweak to her life, resulting in an equally dramatic cure.

This lady came for help with IBS (Irritable Bowel Syndrome). She was a single mum working a full-time job, so as you can imagine, her life was pretty full. She knew something had to change, but as she said to me "I'm not in control of anything, my baby takes priority in my life and I can't afford to lose my job, there isn't any time for me, there is nothing I can do about it" *(notice the 'all or nothing' thinking).* On her fourth session she arrived a different person, she was bubbly and happy and full of energy, a complete contrast to the exhausted emotional client of early weeks. I said to her "You are a different person this week, what changed?" "Nothing" she said, "I just feel better and my IBS has cleared up."

"Why?" I asked.

She went on to explain that all she had done was started leaving work on time. The only change was fifteen minutes of her day. Instead of leaving late at 4.45pm, she left on time at 4.30pm. This meant that she missed the worst of the traffic and got to her child minder on time instead of late and stressed. When she picked up her baby she was more relaxed and so, instead of having a screaming 18 month old in the car all the way home, the journey was relaxed and she was able to interact calmly with her daughter. They both arrived home less stressed and so she became more engaged in the moment with dinner time, enjoying time with her daughter, she started to look forward to the bedtime routine and telling stories instead of dreading the tantrums, and because she was more relaxed her baby slept better – so she slept better. The next morning she woke feeling more refreshed and the whole morning routine was calm and she arrived at work on time instead of rushed.

But the most surprising result for her was the positive effect it had on work. When she was at her worst, she was constantly worried that she would be judged as a single mum juggling responsibilities and her performance at work would deteriorate. So she was staying late just to get it all cleared up and it looked as if she was putting in the time even though she was a single mum. But her work was deteriorating because of the stress she was putting herself under. Shortly after she made the decision to leave on time, her performance improved, she was more able to focus, more proactive and returned to the happy fun work colleague she was before and she enjoyed being at work instead of resenting it.

All she had done was adjust her day by fifteen minutes, but she had made a change that changed her life.

The third client also had an eating disorder and she came for help because her and her boyfriend wanted to get married and start a family, but she didn't want to pass the unhealthy attitude towards food she had developed at seven years old on to her children. She was a lovely client to work with, she went through all the processes she needed to and made lots of changes in her life, she got more involved in social activities with friends, took up netball as a sport, resolved some leadership issues at work where she had been promoted to a manager, and as the weeks went on she noticed many improvements to herself and her confidence, but the eating disorder hadn't gone. She felt braver about tackling it and wanted to, but it was still there.

Week 12 she came in with a big smile on her face, it was just after Christmas and she had figured something out -

She realised that she had been resenting her fiancé for not doing the things she thought he should do to show her that he loves her. She had opened her eyes to what he was doing that previously she hadn't appreciated; for him they were big gestures. She was so fixed on what he wasn't doing that she missed what he was doing.

For this client the change needed was a mindset shift. She needed to let go of trying to control things that weren't hers to control – in her case, her boyfriend's displays of affection. But this was just a catalyst, it flowed into other areas of her life, when she let go of control in other areas, the lifelong eating disorder disappeared.

Incidentally eating disorders are always about control, especially in children. Children are not in control of much in their life, but they are always in control of what they put in their mouth. But for this client, the cure wasn't getting control of her eating, it was letting go of control of other things.

What these examples demonstrate is that the solution is not in the problem; it never is.

Finally as further proof that the solution is not in the problem, the solution is in changing something. Another client came to see me wanting to stop eating chocolate.

The problem had got out of hand to the extent that she was secretly stealing chocolate from her children and hated herself for it. She was an intelligent lady who chose to put her career on the back burner while the children were young. But her youngest child was now 16 years old. She worked out that she was unfulfilled intellectually and decided to go to University as a mature student and get a degree. She still likes chocolate, but she can go into a shop now without buying five bars of it.

The chocolate was not the problem, it was just a warning sign that something else wasn't right in her life and this is usually the case.

Your job is to get your life balanced and create sufficient levels of serotonin and dopamine so your intellectual brain will work out what needs to change.

It will work it out, you just have to feed it serotonin and get out of its way.

# Chapter 26 – Life Balance

We all need to find and maintain a balance in our lives. It's not necessarily equal and it's not the same for everyone, but you do need your balance. When you are deciding what is most effectively going to create serotonin and dopamine for you, taking a look at your life balance is a good starting point.

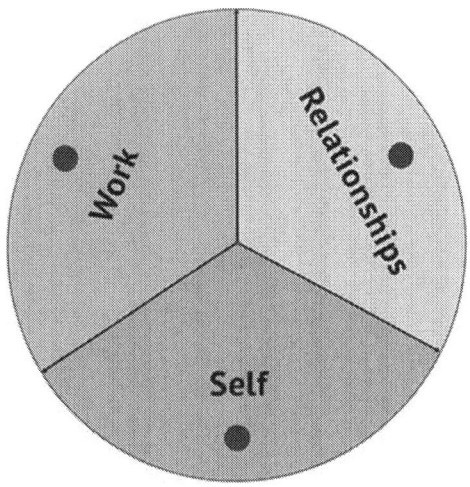

There are three areas you need to consider

You could think of it like those ball bearing games with each section having its own ball bearing that you have to carefully and delicately balance into the hole and then keep that one there while you work on getting the next one in, and so on.

What tends to happen is that we get everything balanced, life is good and we're happy living on Cloud 9, then we put the balancing game down on the sideboard and forget to check in that everything is OK.

Something or someone comes along to dislodge one of the ball bearings – perhaps it's work or maybe a relationship with someone, but what we immediately do is give that section all our attention and focus. We are so focused on getting that particular ball bearing back in the hole, we ignore everything else and, before we know it, we are completely off balance again, heading on a downhill spiral towards depression, hell-bent on getting the problem ball bearing under control.

The solution is NOT in the problem, it never is.

The secret to rebalancing is getting the 'self' ball bearing back in first by doing the positives things that create serotonin and then the other two will fall into place easily.

Stepping back and focusing on yourself when you're fighting with a partner or work is particularly stressful is the hardest thing to do, partly because you think you will drop the problem ball bearing if you step back from it, but equally because we think it is selfish to put your own needs first.

---

**NEWSFLASH**

Putting your own needs first is

NOT selfish - it is selfless

---

We are taught that it is selfish to put ourselves first, but this is often misinterpreted or misunderstood. Someone who only thinks about themselves and doesn't give any consideration to other people could be considered selfish, but this is not the same as looking after your own needs.

Only you can look after your own needs. People who care about you will tell you that "you need to do this" or "you should do that", but only you can make the decisions and actually do something for yourself.

The reason looking after your own needs is selfless not selfish is because when you are looking after your own needs, you are balanced, you feel good, you have the right chemical balance and life balance. Then and only then you are in the best place to look after the other people you need or want to.

You cannot just give and give and give if you are not right yourself, you need to be in a good place first.

Think of the emergency safety instructions you hear before any flight takes off. You are told to put your own oxygen mask on first BEFORE you help others, even young children. If you run out of oxygen, you can't help anyone.

Your wellbeing is exactly the same, you have to look after yourself first as a priority, then you can look after others.

When you give to other people, but quietly resent them for it, then that is selfish – how do they know you are so drained yourself you don't have the personal resources to keep giving? Some people even go as far as insisting on giving, even when someone says there is no need, because they've decided that the other person needs their help – they then get stressed at the time it takes out of their day and resent the person who they insisted on helping.

Look after your own needs and you will become happy to give selflessly.

Looking after yourself as a priority is as vital, as becoming aware of your triggers, early warning signs and effective solutions for the very unique you is the secret to living on Cloud 9.

I have a tattoo on my right wrist, where I see it every day, it says

## "Memento Vivere"

which means "Remember to Live"

I'm not suggesting everyone gets tattoos, but the reason I had it done was to remind me to get a life and live. I have a tendency to work too much and become too focused on work. I love my work, I'm very passionate about it, but it can take over my life if I don't keep a check on the balances in my life.

When I start working too much, I stop looking after my own needs and my serotonin levels drop. It generally takes about two weeks for me to notice I've dropped if I ignore my intuition screaming at me and let it go too far. The areas I compromise for work are socialising and exercise (running).

When this happens, I deliberately arrange to see friends or I arrange social engagements and activities. I don't want to at the time, I want to work because I've become focused on something in particular and I'm determined to fix something or get a piece of work finished that I'm struggling with. However, I know that I'm not as focused as I should be, I know deep down that I'm procrastinating and I'm easily distracted, I'm cutting corners, I'm not putting 100% effort in when I am working and the results are not my best work – I know this and I'm annoyed at myself.

The answer is NOT to work harder.

The answer is to put it down and go and have some fun.

When I return to it, I'm refreshed, refocused, sharper and I have new inspiration and energy.

Focusing on the problem is not the solution – it never is.

I have to constantly remind myself to have fun. When we are not doing the things we think we should, we punish ourselves with not having fun, we don't think we deserve it, so we do nothing at all.

Having fun and enjoying yourself will create serotonin – guaranteed, then and only then will you feel more motivated to do the things you need to do.

Of course you do need discipline in your life – but it's a balance.

# Exercise 9 – How Balanced Is Your Life

Write a list of what you do in a typical week and attach a time value to it.

There are 168 hours in a week, you should be getting 56 hours sleep a week, leaving 112 hours you need to account for.

(If you are sleeping more than 56 hours, you need to introduce more discipline about being awake. You may be exhausted initially, but you won't turn things around until you spend more time creating serotonin.)

Then go through that list and put each thing into one of the categories

- **Work**
- **Relationships**
- **Self**

Next add up the time you spend in each segment and have a look at it – does anything jump out at you?

If you are spending an hour commuting to work, it goes under the "work" segment. But, if you are spending the time during the commute listening to self development audiobooks or something similar you enjoy that engages your mind, you can put it under "self".

If you take an hour for lunch and meet friends, not talking about work, put it in "relationships". If you do something for yourself or exercise, it goes in "self". If you work through lunch or spend lunch time talking about work – it goes in "work " (and put yourself on the naughty step).

Make a positive intention to rebalance yourself and your life. If there's a large portion of TV watching in there, commit to changing some of that time to doing something more productive; giving your brain something positive to do.

# Chapter 27 – Basic Human Needs

I would recommend a book by Joe Griffin and Ivan Tyrell call 'The Human Givens' (recommended reading list) that explains how humans have certain fundamental psychological and emotional needs.

These needs fall into two broad categories – Purpose and Relationships.

## Purpose

We all need a purpose in life – a reason to get out of bed in the morning. Once our basic needs for safety, food and shelter are satisfied, what motivates us? For some it is being a parent, for others it's their job or the work they do in the community. Work is important, but this isn't necessarily traditional 'paid' work, by work I mean 'doing something that contributes'.

Contributes to what? 'What' it contributes to isn't necessarily important, but it should be something that makes you feel valued, it could be your family, your community, mankind ….

## Relationships

We also need to know where we fit in within our intimate relationships, our families, friends, social circle, work colleagues and communities. We need a role within those relationships and we need to feel that we're accepted and we fit in. For humans, fitting into the tribe means survival and safety.

When we are displaced from our normal purpose or relationships our anxiety levels rise. You will remember that when anxiety rises, the primitive brain steps in and takes control, thinking there is some sort of crisis, emergency or danger. The primitive brain always works within the parameters of anxiety, depression and anger – or a combination of all three.

If you were actually in those primitive times and you were displaced from your tribe or unable to carry out your purpose for some reason, you would probably be in a life-threatening situation. Of course, it isn't life-threatening today, but your blueprint hasn't changed and your primitive brain doesn't know that.

When we have life changing events and the status quo is upset, for those who are worrying about the future and what might happen, anxiety can become overwhelming, and those who negatively introspect about themselves, their lives and what they have lost become depressed.

I see this happening frequently on the island I live on. Many couples retire to the island and for a period of time everything is wonderful; they've been looking forward to "not having to work" for years and life is an exciting new start in a beautiful place.

However, after the "honeymoon period" or when the excitement and novelty of being on an island and not working wears off, some people become depressed or develop symptoms of anxiety because they have disrupted their status quo and not rebalanced with a new one.

And they are confused by this – "Why am I depressed? I have all the time in the world to do things, I don't have to work any more, I live on a beautiful island in the sun, so why do I feel so miserable?"

Both areas of their fundamental human needs have changed and until they replace them and create their new purpose and relationships, their primitive brain is going to carry on believing there is a crisis, emergency or danger.

Even in retirement, people still need to find a purpose and a reason for getting up in the morning. Life has changed, but that need hasn't suddenly gone, we need to adapt and change with life's ever changing circumstances.

Even though they made the choice to move abroad, they are still displaced from their friends, family and the community they know in a new environment with new people, they need to build new relationships and find their place and role within this new community.

Traditionally people would have stayed within the same community and their role would have naturally progressed through very clearly defined parameters. As people become too old to hunt or do hard physical labour, they became 'elders', people respected for their wisdom and knowledge. When women were past child-bearing age, they had a valued role in helping their daughters with childcare and had other valuable skills to contribute to the family and community.

In modern society those traditional roles have become blurred, the natural tribal support networks have all but disappeared and new life changing circumstances have emerged.

Divorce, moving house to a new area, changing job, children leaving home, coping with a new baby on your own, retirement, redundancy or not having a job, they all disrupt the status quo of our basic human psychological and emotional needs.

## So what do we do about it?

To be blunt - you get up off your backside and start addressing these needs – without coming up with negative excuses for why you can't.

I'm not completely heartless, I do understand that if you've had depression for a long time you will have lost confidence, energy and motivation and maybe you are not at the stage yet where you have sufficient serotonin to do some of these things. Go back and study Part 2 to understand how you create serotonin until you are at the level where your intellectual brain kicks in and works out how you're going to fulfill these needs.

Most importantly, you know you need to do this, so set yourself a positive intention that you are going to find new (whatever you need to do) and your brain will work out the rest – get out of its way.

# Chapter 28 – Social Life and Interests

Have you ever noticed how much more sociable you are when you're in a good place emotionally, physically and happy?

It is no coincidence that you meet significant people in your life when you are at your best.

Depression and loneliness are co-conspirators. People need to be with people, it's in our blueprint, so when we don't have enough interaction with our own kind, our serotonin and dopamine levels drop, resulting in a lack of motivation to go out and meet people and we become lonely.

When life circumstances change you may find yourself displaced from your 'tribe', your family, friends, social circle and communities.

It's sad that some people believe that their depression will magically disappear when they find someone special to be with. The truth is they will find someone special when they are out of depression.

Of course I am talking about partners and someone to love, but equally I'm talking about friends in general.

Someone who is depressed is hard work to be around. They are negative, complain about everything, talk about themselves and their problems constantly and bring everything back to being about them - they are having their own pity party and are looking for other people to join in.

Or they can't get motivated to go out and be with people, instead they complain that no one ever contacts them or visits.

When you have depression, you inadvertently push people away, it's hard work and not much fun for other people to be around you and, as well as that, a habit of a depressed person is to think negatively about other people, so they will look for faults and problems in other people, focus on what their friends are NOT doing – but they don't tell them, they just believe their own negative imagined reasons why and cut friends out of their life.

People like to be around people who are happy, relaxed, calm, easy to be around and fun.

So you have two jobs:-

1. Work on your own self-development so you become the relaxed, happy, calm person who is easy to be with, ie get yourself out of depression.
2. Go out and get yourself a social life – it is up to YOU to create your social life. It isn't going to come knocking on your door.

When you start doing the positive self development things in your life that create serotonin – Positive Thinking, Positive Interaction and Positive Activity – you will also become naturally more confident and you will find that you attract people to you without any effort on your part. You will also feel braver and more able to step out of your comfort zone and try new things, which is exactly what you need to do in order to create even more serotonin.

If you want to meet someone special and attract a new lover or partner into your life, you will do it without even trying when you are the best you can be, happy, relaxed and calm.

Until you are better, you will continue to follow the same patterns as always with your relationships. It is not everyone else who needs to change; it is you, from the inside out.

It's not unusual for clients to make statements along the lines of;

>"I don't know what I like"

>"I don't have any interests"

>"I'm doing the things I used to like, but they don't excite me any more"

>"I can't do the things I like because …"

When you are looking at the problems all the time, of course you're not going to be able to work out what you like or might like. If your life circumstances have changed significantly and you can no longer do the things you used to do or be with the people you used to spend time with, it's challenging to know what to do.

>You only know what you know.

How do you discover new things to do and like?

How do you meet people who are like you that you will have a natural rapport with?

You put yourself in situations that increase your opportunities to meet them. This means doing the things you enjoy and you will meet others who like the same things.

I discovered a passion for sailing completely by chance by trying something new.

When I separated from my husband in 2012, I needed to create a life as a single person again and I felt I desperately needed to get away and have a holiday. However, all my close friends were married, in relationships and had children. I had been taking groups trekking in the Himalayas for the last eight years, which I loved, but I wanted to be near the sea in the sunshine and take a holiday where I was not responsible for anyone else.

When I was depressed the first time, I did go on a beach resort holiday in Greece on my own – honestly, it was miserable, I felt like Billy No Mates all week. I wasn't in the right place to do that emotionally, I wasn't yet out of the depression really and I kept myself to myself, at that time I didn't have the confidence to be sociable.

I didn't want to repeat that experience so I tried another strategy. Many of the people on the trekking groups I organised came on their own and, as we were a group, it was always friendly and sociable and we had a great time, so I started looking for group activity holidays. I didn't want to book on a 'singles' holiday, that came with expectations and pressure and I wasn't ready to get into a new relationships, so I looked at something I knew I would be OK with - yoga retreats; "get healthy" I thought.

I came across many yoga retreats that also offered other activities and it dawned on me that I was checking out the dates for yoga retreats that also offered sailing as an extra activity and I realised that it was in fact sailing I wanted to try.

So I switched my search to Cabin Charters.

To cut a long story short, I had an amazing holiday, I met a lovely bunch of people, everyone had to be sociable, we were all stuck on a boat with a bunch of strangers with a common interest; becoming friends was easy.

Just four years on and I have loads of lovely sailing friends. I had no idea how much my life would change at the time, but that small act of making the decision to step outside my comfort zone and try something new was the seed that grew into a whole new life. I now live on an island in the Mediterranean and next year I will be living on a yacht (and working from it) – four years ago I lived in the middle of the UK and I didn't even know how to sail.

I had a hypnotherapy client who came to see me for general anxiety. He was a lovely guy, but the worst workaholic I had ever come across, I would have said he had OCD about work. But I didn't need to point out that he needed a better work/life balance, he already knew that, unfortunately however, his social anxiety held him back; he hadn't socialised for so long, he didn't know how to any more.

But he worked out that if he booked himself on evening classes he would have to leave work earlier those nights, he would be around other people outside work who were all in the same boat of meeting new people for the first time and he might even discover a new interest or passion.

He tried many different things, languages, art, archaeology, I don't know how he chose what he wanted to study but the way he put it was to use the analogy of a bowling alley.

He said, "if I throw enough balls at the pins, eventually I'm going to get a strike".

And he did, he discovered he had a passion for archaeology, so he booked on digs as a volunteer and created a social life that he loved.

Having an online social life isn't enough, you need to get out and be with other people, it is essential for your mental health.

Of course it is scary, your primitive brain is going to try and stop you stepping outside your comfort zone at all costs, but you can overrule it, feel the fear and do it anyway.

The internet is a valuable resource for finding new things to get involved with that you can do alone

- Local evening classes
- Volunteering
- Meetup.com

The last one, meetup.com is a site that brings like-minded people together and you can even organise a group get-together for something you would like to do.

Getting involved in activities for the first time is a daunting prospect, but other people are usually very friendly and welcoming and have all been in the position of going along alone for the first time themselves.

There will be other similar websites and social groups local to you. The more you are with other people, the more serotonin and dopamine you are creating and the less time you spend by yourself thinking too much.

# Exercise 10 – Brainstorm & Research

What do you like to do?

If you could introduce something new in your life, what would it be?

- Education – Learn something new
- Hobbies, passions and interests
- Volunteering, getting involved with community projects

Get a large piece of paper and write down anything you can think of, no matter how extreme you think it is.

Go on the internet and start a google search and see where that takes you, the key is to be aware of what your brain is locking on to.

What interests do you lean towards, health, fashion, travel, the sea, mountains, textiles, crafts.

Remember you don't have to make any life decisions about what you're going to do next immediately and it doesn't matter if you don't like the first thing you try. The idea is to practice stepping outside your comfort zone and doing something new.

You will meet other people along the way who introduce you to other things, ideas and people and perhaps take you off in directions you hadn't previously considered. You just have to start the ball rolling by trying something different.

# Chapter 29 – Subconscious Wiring

Let's return to science for a moment and learn another strategy that you can proactively practice. Your mind cannot hope to consciously contemplate everything you're exposed to during a day, you are bombarded with information from all your senses and if it were to attempt manual processing of this information, you would become completely overwhelmed and go just a little bit mad! Your subconscious mind selectively brings your attention to what you need to know; it knows what you need to know because you've told it by how you think.

Have you ever noticed how, when something important is happening in your life, it also seems to be happening everywhere and to everybody at the same time; for example when you were pregnant, getting married or bought a new car (not necessarily in that order), there seemed to be babies or weddings everywhere and suddenly everybody has the same car as you – coincidence? No!

You had told your brain to bring to your conscious attention anything to do with that thing currently important in your life.

There is a part of your brain called the basal ganglia that is responsible for setting the parameters of the filters in your brain. As babies these filters have not been set, but very quickly the brain learns what is normal that the subconscious can deal with and what is important enough to alert your conscious mind. Throughout our lives we are constantly adapting, tweaking and changing these filters, depending on what's important to us right at that moment.

When you have practiced thinking negatively for a while, you will have reset the parameter of the filters in the basal ganglia to filter in negative stuff from the sense and the environment or what's happening around you. Have you ever thought, "my glass is half empty" or "shit always happens to me"? It's not, but you are noticing all the negative things above everything else because you've told you brain to notice.

You also have your own central sorting office, called the thalamus, your senses, sight, hearing, smell, touch and taste all bring information to the central sorting office via the filters. Then it's the job of the sorting office to decide what to do with that information. Does it send it to the emergency response room because it's something that has been tagged as a potential threat, does it dismiss it as irrelevant to your needs, does it send it to your subconscious to be stored away for later use? Or does it bring it to the attention of your conscious brain?

You are subconsciously in control of the sorting office by how you think.

Do you think of yourself as a lucky or unlucky person, is your glass half full or half empty?

Until I learned how this worked, I had always thought of myself as a lucky person, my glass was half full, I was known for falling in the proverbial poo, but coming up smelling of roses. It pleased me that I was a lucky person and I accepted it.

When I had my spell of depression, I thought 'luck' had left me, everything had turned unlucky in my life. It hadn't, my mindset had shifted to negative.

However, these days I don't believe in luck at all because I now know that we are all in control of our own luck. Everyone has the power or opportunity to be lucky or unlucky - it is choice, thought patterns and perception.

Of course nobody would rationally choose to be unlucky (although I do come across people who seem to relish in being a "glass half empty" person), most people are not aware of how they are directly affecting their own "luck" and life, just as I wasn't aware I was choosing to be lucky.

Nonetheless it is a choice. You choose how you think at a subconscious level and if that is not working for you right now, you can retrain it.

You do this by understanding that what you think about sets the parameters of the filters and instructs the sorting office about how to handle the incoming information.

You can reset this at a subconscious level to start working in your favour.

If you have spent many years wiring your brain for negativity, you will need to retrain your brain, but this can be done easily, it just takes consistency and practice.

The more you retrain your thinking to be positive and let go of the negative inhibitions which hold you back, the quicker your mind will let go of the negative neural pathways.

As you practice, it is important to genuinely think in a positive way and not with the negative verb, for example

- "It's going to be a lovely sunny day tomorrow," Instead of "it's not going to rain"
- "I'm going to have a productive day today," instead of "I'm not going to procrastinate and waste time"

It's also important not to build opt-out clauses and caveats into your thinking, for example:-

*"I'll apply for a new job, when the right thing comes up".*

How is your brain to know when the right thing comes up if you haven't told it what that is? You need to take action and put in the work to give your brain some guidelines of what that is, instead of building in opt-out clauses for doing nothing.

You might reply "I will know when it does". You might be waiting a very long time. You might not know this instance what the right thing is, but you can still give your brain positive instructions and take positive action towards your goals and in this way you take control and you make luck happen.

Your brain is incredibly powerful, beyond anything we can understand at the moment, it will come up with answers for you, but it needs to know what you do want, not what you don't want.

So a much more productive way is thinking about how you would like things to be.

*"I'm going to get a new job, what sort of thing would I like to do or what is out there that I can apply for?"*

The question is almost the same, you need a job but you don't know what. However there is a subtle but significant difference, and that difference is you have just given your brain the positive instruction to look at something.

In that moment of positive decision you have changed the filters and instructed the sorting office in a positive way that will bring you opportunities you might be interested in. It starts a whole chain reaction of events in your brain that you have started with a positive thought. You will start to mention during conversations with friends that you're looking for a new job and they will provide input that could take you down a completely new thought path and trigger thought patterns that consider possibilities you may not have thought about before.

You have just opened up your life and possibilities instead of shut it down which was your previous modus operandi.

This way of thinking has nothing to do with <u>waiting</u> for the right thing to come up, it has everything to do with <u>making</u> the right thing come up. You put yourself in control of your destiny instead of waiting for the destiny to happen to you.

Putting caveats on your thinking is equally unhelpful.

*"I will get fit when I can find a time to go to the gym."*

In the statement above you haven't decided to find time, it's a statement of your subconscious intent not go to the gym.

*"When I can afford it, When I have time, I will when…"*

are all caveats ensuring it's not going to happen. Maybe it is not the right time right now, but adding a "when" something else has happened is not solidifying any intent, it is inserting an intentional delay. If it is genuinely bad timing right now a better subconscious statement would be:

*"In January I'm going to change jobs, I'll start applying in November and in the meantime I'm going to look at what I would like to do now."*

These examples all show the difference between giving your mind something positive to do and putting up barriers to doing anything.

People who are perceived as lucky are lucky because they open up the filters and allow opportunities to be filtered in purely because they think in a positive way.

People who think positively have ideas and opportunities coming at them all the time, which they then consider and decide to let go or follow through.

People who perceive themselves as unlucky are doing the exact opposite, their negative thinking habits are blocking opportunities and ideas or dismissing them because they look for the negative consequences instead of the possible positive outcomes.

The same amount of good and bad things happens to everybody. The difference is how the parameters of the filters have been set by the way that person thinks.

Who would choose to be the negative person?

It doesn't make any rational sense to do that, does it?

Your subconscious needs to know your intentions, without any ambiguity, caveat or opt-out clauses and then it can start working towards your goals.

## Rewiring Your Subconscious

It is said that we have to routinely practice something 11 times before it becomes habit.

The saying "practice makes perfect" is a little ambiguous, it implies that you get a very good at what you practice and I would agree, you do; but it doesn't define whether the way you are practicing is a right or wrong, so you could be very good at doing something badly if you practice it that way.

A more accurate statement might be "practice makes permanent", so if you practice something regularly however you are doing it - that's what will stick.

This is also true of how you practice thinking. If you have practiced negativity, that will be your habit.

You already know that changing habits and establishing better ones can take some concentration and persistence. There is an easy way to do this that starts with changing routines and becoming aware of triggers.

As we grow up we build up a database of associations in our mind, a bit like playing 'snap' in our head with a huge pack of life cards. When we turn over a card it will trigger associations and actions and we unconsciously follow a set of preprogrammed instructions.

People close to you may well know your habits and instruction sets better than you do. If you talk to couples who have been together for many years they will know each other's routines inside out.

This isn't a bad thing - we can't go throughout our day consciously thinking about every step or action we take - but if we have become stuck in negative patterns and want to change, we can help this process by changing our routines.

It doesn't have to be anything big - just switching the order in which we do something could be enough to give us a conscious jolt out of the automatic and form new associations and positive habits.

For example if you are trying to think in a more positive way, there are several things you can easily change that will jolt you out of your routine thinking, for example:-

- Change the order of your morning routine
- Get up at a different time and do something else first, meditate first perhaps.
- On your way to work listen to podcasts or audiobooks that you have to actively engage with instead of having the radio or background music on.

- Go away from your desk or workplace at lunchtime. Go for a walk, meet friends or do something different.
- On your way home from work do something different - pop in and see a friend perhaps.
- Change your routine in the evening. This is one of the downtimes where we have too much negative thinking time. Just because you've always got home and had dinner first, it doesn't mean that's how you always have to do it.

Everything is completely within your control. The choices you make determine how your life pans out, it's up to you to make different choices if you are not happy in life.

The significance of changing those routines is in the subtle disconnection of automatic thought patterns and associations that are linked to habits. So if you have decided to practice thinking in a positive way, changing your habits will give you a conscious poke back to thinking positively when you're about to slip back to thinking negatively.

Over time the new routines become associated with positive thinking and the positive thinking creates serotonin so you get rewarded with enjoying your new routines as new associations settle in and become unconscious habits.

# Chapter 30 – Creating Reality from Imagination

Dare to dream– what does that mean to you?

We use our imagination constantly, but often we're not aware we are doing it. Becoming aware of when your imagination is in play and what is reality is a vital skill in regaining control over your mind.

Skill may seem a strange expression to use, but it is something we have to learn to do, then practice. Much of the time we are unconscious of when our imagination is taking over and we believe it to be true. You need to develop the habit of noticing your imagination and accepting it for what it is. Or, turn it around and use this knowledge to your advantage.

You can take positive control and use your imagination to enhance your life and improve your skills by practicing them in your mind.

Many top sportsmen and women understand very well the importance of practicing their skills in their mind.

A top golfer will go over and over a shot in his or her mind, visualising the golf ball flying through the air in the exact trajectory and distance intended, landing inperfectly.

A sprinter or runner will see themselves finishing first and breaking through the tape.

A boxer will practice in their mind routines and set pieces, as will an ice skater, a dancer, an actor, or a musician.

Practicing something in your mind is as good as the thing itself.

You already know this as well. When you are trying to remember something, going over and over it in your mind will imprint it to your memory. As you practice something in your mind you form and strengthen neural networks.

You can actively and consciously take your imagination and put it to work for you, deciding to believe in a future you want to create, for example.

If you decide that within the next two years, you will have a new job, double your current salary and be driving that new car you have always wanted, you will make it happen.

You are using your imagination and simultaneously dropping the caveats and opt-outs, resetting the parameters in your mind to filter in relevant opportunities that your sorting office it will know to bring to your conscious attention.

You are already creating reality from your imagination on a daily basis, but perhaps this has been in a negative way until now.

When someone has depression, they think in terms of

*"it's really hard fighting depression"*

They have just created their own living reality. Because they believe it to be hard – it is exactly that.

How powerful would it be if you could do the opposite and create the reality you want if you switch your thinking 180 degrees to positive?

## You can.

# Exercise 11 – Creating Your Preferred Future

As you work through this exercise remember to use your imagination in a positive way and phrase your desires in terms of what you DO want and not what you DON'T want.

What you imagine you want right now will change, allow that to happen. This exercise is a daily and weekly practice, as you become more attuned to focusing on a positive future, what you believe you can achieve will expand and what you believe you want will change, this is very normal. Invite change, ambition and new beliefs into your life.

1. What three things that you did last week are you most pleased about?

2. What three things show you that you are working towards you goals?

3. What are your Top 3 Goals within the next year?

4. What are your Top 3 Goals within the next 5 years?

5. What are your Top 3 Goals for the next 3 months?

6. What are your Top 3 Goals this month?

7. What are your Top 3 Goals this week?

8. What are you going to do today that works towards your goals this week?

No 8 should be revisited on a daily basis whilst 1-7 are weekly tasks, do this exercise on a Sunday morning.

# Chapter 31 – Your Subconscious Superpowers

You have superpowers!

Look at some of the incredible things humans have achieved – we can fly around the world, we can breath underwater, we can create light where there is dark, we can communicate with each other over thousands of miles in nano seconds, we can replace parts of our bodies that are worn out with new ones and we've even walked on the moon for goodness sake!

Yep, you can do anything you want to and you can make anything happen that you want to.

But remember, your personal superpowers are restricted to being superhero superpowers, they only work when used with positive intention

So, for example, you cannot use your superpower to control someone else or what they are thinking or doing, that would be a villain superpower; you can only use your superpower to make positive things happen and bring happiness to yourself and others.

I have already touched on using your imagination to create your reality and how you programme your mind to filter in or out information depending on the way you think. Along the same lines is focus.

Whatever you focus on will increase, so if you focus on your problems, they will increase, focusing on what you don't have will repel it even more which is why you need to focus on the things you want to bring into your life.

You cannot tell yourself to NOT focus on something because your brain will only focus on the object in question, so if you say you don't want any more bills to arrive, inevitably more bills will arrive through the letterbox.

This is very evident with sleeping. If you go to bed worrying about not being able to sleep – what happens? And if you tell yourself to not worry about not sleeping – what happens?

Maintaining happiness is the practice of setting positive intentions and engineering the life you really want.

Forget what you believe is or isn't possible. If you think something is impossible, you will be right, so if you want to switch your superpowers on, you have to learn to drop preconceived ideas of what is or isn't possible.

There is a quote from Henry Ford that goes

**"Whether you think you can or you think you can't, you're right"**

Learning to use this knowledge without creating doubt, caveats or opt-out clauses is the secret to tapping into your superpower.

You can engineer your life to be exactly how you want it to be, you just need to believe it and then you make it happen.

Walt Disney is quoted as saying

## "If you can dream it, you can do it."

That statement backs up what I have been saying about using your imagination in a positive way to create your future.

All these things are true and, if I may, I would like to tell you the true story about how my life has changed since learning how to operate my brain properly.

Before I begin, I'm not sharing this with you for any boastful or self serving purposes, I'm sharing it as a demonstration of what you can do for yourself and your life with positive intention. I'm sure there are people who have bigger and more interesting stories and I'm also not suggesting you need to do what I've done, you need to follow a path that is right by you, but turn on your superpowers and you can achieve anything.

As I revealed at the beginning of this book, I first got knocked sideways by depression in 2002, then subsequently relapsed in 2010 all set to follow the same patterns of behaviour because I didn't understand my contribution to the cause of depression or even that I was responsible, let alone have any tools or techniques to bringing myself out of depression. Both times I bounced back by making major changes in my life.

The second time I made a decision to retrain, no matter how long it took; I was going to do it. My best friend suggested I should train as a counselor, I didn't have any better ideas and I trusted her judgment more than mine at that time, so I enrolled on a course.

I won't go into why, it's not relevant, but I decided counselling wasn't for me, however, during the course of the Level 1 Counselling, hypnotherapy was mentioned (and dismissed) but I was curious, I had never heard of it before, so I started looking for courses.

I discovered a professional course in Bristol at The Clifton Practice and applied. Within two weeks I had been interviewed, accepted and started on the course.

On the very first day, I experienced hypnosis myself for the first time. I was a bit skeptical and scared of letting go of control of my mind, exactly the same as everyone is the first time, but I needn't have worried, you don't actually relinquish control of your mind, you are in control all the time, it was just a lovely uplifting experience.

But what changed my life was a paragraph from the script the lecturer used that went like this:-

*"Whenever you allow your conscious mind to become focused on your problems, you drag your problems into the future with you and they automatically attract still more of the same. Your own negative thought patterns provide the psychic energies that feed your problems and keep them alive. So just relax and switch the polarity around and focus your thought energy on how you want things to be, rather than how you don't want them to be and withdraw all your thought energy from the problems, so that you attract the solutions. You attract good fortune like a magnet. The control mind now knows what you want and what you want, or something even more useful, presents itself, as though what you have been always seeking has, somehow, always been seeking you,*

*seeking to find creative expression in your everyday living reality, and the incredible fact is, that it has.*

*"So, make a moving picture in your mind, a picture of you as you see yourself having accomplished all the desired changes. The unwanted patterns of behaviour have ceased. Everything is exactly as you want it to be, see it, feel it, know it, experience it. Everything, just as you want it to be....the picture becoming clearer, brighter, bigger. The new picture dominates the screen. Leave the picture in the mirror of the mind to serve as an attracting force, and it will – just want it to happen, know it can happen, it happens. You struggled with your problems in the past and tried to outrun the shadow of your past conditioning; now you can relax. Just relax and create the attracting force from the stillness and be amazed at the quality of the success you attract."*

Remember that I knew nothing about any of this, it was my first day on the course, I had never been hypnotised before and, to be honest, if you knew me, you would know that I don't believe in much that's considered "fluffy", I'm very much logical, practical and science-based.

However, when that second paragraph started with "make a moving picture in your mind" the image that popped into my mind was of me standing next to a grey Audi TT sports car. I knew several things without a doubt from that picture, a) I was happy, b) I was single and c) it was MY car.

After the session, we went to lunch, I did feel on my Cloud 9, but I forgot about the image from the script.

At that particular time I was married, broke, overweight and a smoker. I had taken a loan to pay for the course to retrain and I didn't have a flash sports car, so the image was more amusing than believable as a future reality.

Less than a year later, I was single, I had a brand new Audi TT, had stopped smoking, lost two stone in weight and was Living on Cloud 9.

But that's not all that has happened since.

Two years on from that I was running a very successful hypnotherapy practice in Swindon, I had another hypnotherapist working with me to cope with the workload I was generating – right from day one of training, it didn't even cross my mind that I wouldn't be successful as a hypnotherapist, I just believed I would without question. What I didn't appreciate at the time was that most of my counterparts struggled to find clients after qualifying, the opposite was happening to me.

It was December and I was having a birthday drink in a pub with my best friend (yes, the same one responsible for starting off down this path) I was feeling a bit restless about my life and I asked her,

*"If you moved out of Swindon, where would you move to?"*

*"I don't think I would"*, she said *"but if I did, it would probably be Brighton".*

*"Yes, I like Brighton"* I agreed.

This planted the seed and I started thinking about moving. We continued the conversation and I said

*"I would love to move to Brighton, but it's probably a year or more away for me being able to do that"*

Just four months later, the following April, I moved to Brighton and Hove and started a second branch of Old Town Hypnotherapy.

I loved living in Brighton and Hove, it's a great place, but it didn't end there.

I loved being a hypnotherapist and I love helping people to make positive changes in their lives, but there are two drawbacks for me, the first is that it's a fixed location. When you take a new client, you are committed to that client for 8-12 weeks and of course it's a rolling programme of new clients and you can't just leave them and go away or hand them on to someone else, you need to see through their treatment with them. Secondly, as a hypnotherapist you are paid per hour, so if you want to earn more, you have to work more and there's an obvious limit to this.

I wanted freedom without limitation in my life, but I had no idea how I could achieve that.

And, that's quite an important point to note – you don't have to know the details of how you are going to achieve something before you start, you just need to start and the path reveals itself as and when it needs to.

Since I was a teenager, I had wanted to live near the Mediterranean, even better be on the sea, messing around on the water. But I had never even considered it as a possible reality; I followed the examples of my parents, family and peers.

But, living by the sea in Hove set me dreaming. I used to say that Brighton and Hove is the closest place you can get in the UK to the culture of living in the Med (what I imagined the Med to be like anyway).

Eight months later, I packed up my house in Hove, put all my belongings in storage and moved to Gozo with no idea whatsoever of how I was going to live beyond the very modest income I earned from franchising Old Town Hypnotherapy.

I've lived here in Gozo for two years now and I love it, I write eBooks and record video courses and run the hypnotherapy businesses as well as my coaching business, all online.

So I have achieved the freedom I dreamed of – but it still doesn't end there.

As I become more confident in my abilities to engineer the life I want, my belief in possibilities expands.

Living on Gozo, I have been able to follow my passion of sailing more regularly and I decided that I wanted to get my own yacht and spend next year sailing around the Greek islands whilst working.

I set my intention and told friends I was on a mission to get a yacht.

One week later I was offered the loan of a 40 ft yacht.

So from depressed, overweight, unhappy, married, stressed and broke having just left my career, to living on a yacht in the Mediterranean, the fittest and healthiest

I've ever been, earning my income from anywhere I want to with just a laptop and internet connection in just five years.

If someone has told me back then that my life would develop in this way, I think I might have laughed in disbelief.

If I had stopped for just one minute to think of what might go wrong, I would never have made the first step and my life would have stayed still.

Everyone has the ability to engineer their own life to exactly how they want it to be, there is nothing special about me at all.

I just opened my mind to learning something new and how to think positively, harness the power of my subconscious to work with me instead of against me and believed in possibilities instead of impossibilities.

What I discovered is that with each small step you make in a direction that is better than before, your self-belief grows. As your self-belief grows, your belief in possibilities grows and you make bigger things happen. It is just a matter of belief.

When you are in alignment, when your conscious brain is working WITH your subconscious, that's when you can make the impossible possible and you will find solutions for whatever you perceive to be wrong in your life right now and you will learn to let go of what you are clinging onto that's holding you back.

If you want or need to redefine your beliefs in what is possible in your life you need to open your mind and fill it with new positive information and thoughts. Your intellect will do the rest, trust it and get out of its way.

## How To Activate Your Subconscious Superpowers

### Do's

- ⇒ Think Positively.
- ⇒ Become self aware of your warning signs and practice early intervention if you are slipping.
- ⇒ Know exactly what creates serotonin for you.
- ⇒ Maintain a healthy life balance.
- ⇒ Focus on what you Do Want.
- ⇒ Let go of what is holding you back.
- ⇒ Open your mind to possibilities.
- ⇒ Use your Imagination to instruct your subconscious of what you do want .
- ⇒ Believe you can and you will achieve whatever you set your mind to.
- ⇒ Take action and step forwards towards your future self and life.
- ⇒ Trust your subconscious. It knows more than you do and it has your interests at heart.

You can beat depression, this is how.

## Don'ts

- × Don't second-guess your intuition or gut feeling, you know the difference between that and negative thinking.

- × Don't get in the way of your intellect, let it do its job, your job is to create serotonin so it can work effectively.

- × Don't listen to naysayers telling you what is or isn't possible, they are advising your purely from their own agenda and experience.

- × Don't ever be fooled into thinking you've got it sussed, you can never stop practicing balancing your life and maintaining your chemical balance.

# Chapter 32 – Summary

Change your attitude towards yourself and depression.

## I can, I will

Or, in the words of Yoda,

> **There is only 'Do' or 'Not Do', there is no 'Try'**

Everyone who has depression, without exception, has a negative attitude and thinks in a negative way. This is what needs to change as a priority because how you think influences your moods, motivation, energy, coping ability and immune system.

It is YOUR brain, so you can do anything you want to do. Retraining your brain is easy, it just takes a bit of self awareness, vigilance and a lot of practice.

Rebalancing your body's chemical composition is fundamental; do this and you WILL change your moods, you WILL create energy and motivation, you WILL feel better. But it's up to you, only you can do it.

The 10 steps to rebalancing your body, mind and emotions are:-

1. Decide without any ambiguity that you ARE going to do this

2. Commit your resolve to a positive affirmation that you can and you will beat depression

3. Become aware of your thought patterns and practice thinking more positively.

4. Start doing small things and congratulate yourself for it, stop beating yourself up for the things you can't do.

5. Put the big problems down, leave them to the universe to deal with, you will not solve a thing by focusing on the problems.

6. Focus on yourself first as a priority, start looking after yourself and do the things you enjoy doing. This is not selfish; it is selfless because when you are better you will have the resources and energy to give to those around you happily and willingly.

7. Make a small step towards your future every day, even if you take a tiny step, keep going and don't stop, however hard it might seem. It's only hard that day because your thoughts have turned negative; tomorrow is a new day. Developing the self-discipline to do this even when you don't want to will bring the biggest rewards.

8. Plan a positive future for yourself, leave the past in the past where it belongs.

9. Eat healthily, you are what you eat. Put crap in and you will feel crap. Put good raw energy in and you will feel energetic.

10. Invest in yourself, you are the most valuable asset in your life, what you know, how you think and what you do will shape your life. Practice self-development.

Your mind is extraordinarily powerful. Science has only touched the surface in understanding our brain, but some things we do know:-

- Your brain is the control centre for your whole mind, body and emotions.

- How you think influences every part of your mind and body, physically and emotionally.

- How you think will determine the outcomes in your daily life.

- There is no right and wrong, there is just belief and it is your choice how and what you believe.

- What you choose to believe will influence your life – positively or negatively.

You won't change a lifetime of habits and beliefs overnight, some things do change quickly because you decide to change your mind, others take time to retrain habits and neural pathways.

I'm still learning what my brain can do, but some things are clear:-

It's exciting discovering what I'm capable of, discarding old beliefs and learning new things. You will be amazed at what you will change your mind about.

The more you practice, the more control you will have over your own mind.

As you practice, your mind becomes even more powerful at bringing the things to you that you need and want. The secret is to focus on what you do want, not on what you don't want.

# Trust Your Intellect and Get Out Of Its Way

# Chapter 33 – The Final Word

I want to leave you with part of an interview I did recently with a guy who reached out to me through Twitter about 18 months ago.

Richard isn't a client, he's not an expert, he's just an ordinary guy with an extraordinary resolve and determination to make his life better.

Richard has brought himself out of depression – he did it himself and I was so inspired by his journey that I asked him if he would do an interview for me.

**Richard, what advice would you give to someone wanting to start their journey out of depression?**

*"I never relied on anyone, I had influences, to borrow a phrase from the Chimp paradox, Emma is a remote part of my troop or for Star Wars fans, my Yoda, but if I don't listen it's a choice, as it is everyone's.*

*TAKING OWNERSHIP IS THE BIGGEST STEP.*

*Getting in touch with my old self was a good step too. Stop being a passenger in your own life, take control, if you cannot surround yourself with positive people, then choose positive people on Facebook or Twitter.*

*Small changes now become big changes in a year's time. Have some "you" time, for me it's time with my dog on the lead in the woods or it used to be fishing."*

**Is there anything you would like to add that you think might help others?**

*I've taken several steps, on your advice I started my own blog that I write almost daily*

*I started running again, giving almost any fitness a go, including yoga, Pilates and general bodyweight training.*

*I can't stress enough the influence that Emma and the book The Chimp Paradox have had, but I did it myself. Like the fool in the Tarot cards or like in Star Wars, 'I chose my own journey'. Who I wanted in my troop which has seen one of my worst influences cut away and not get annoyed when someone didn't want me in their troop.*

*I realised I was free-falling into depression, but to use another vehicle to explain it, I now see myself as the Captain of my ship, Emma (as much as she denies it) is my Navigator and the book my Tactical officer, but I choose what I listen to, what I act upon and what I don't and I know it's MY responsibility if it works or doesn't.*

*The one thing Dad would not have wanted was to hold me back, which for nearly three years he was, I had to let go, I'm not saying I didn't love him, but I hadn't realised what a huge influence he was. He would say what had to be said, but then always had my back.*

*My break-up hurt but I hadn't realised the damage until I met Lou, and she nearly left because I didn't communicate, just boxed everything up which I also now realise wasn't a good thing, either for me or our relationship.*

*Also thinking about it now, I realise that, as Emma has taught me, taking ownership of a problem is a huge step, if you turn around and say "well you told me to......." you can't take the problem on, because you don't own it.*

*If you look at the problem and say to yourself "what, if any part of this, could I change?" you take ownership of it, if you can't change it, then accept, move on and plan how you'll avoid a problem like that, in the future. It maybe a person, it maybe your reaction, it could even be what you're drinking, but you can't do anything until you TAKE OWNERSHIP OF THE PROBLEM.*

*Get in touch with your old self and remember how you used to be. Try doing something you used to enjoy. Sport helps a lot, by burning off adrenaline. Choose your influences, it may not be easy in reality, but it is on Twitter and other social media.*

*I play 'turn the negatives' I enjoy that a lot. A leopard can't change its spots, but it can change the way it sees them!*

*And when someone is giving you a critique they aren't being personal, tell your chimp, "they're not bring rude, let me (your human) deal with this, if I feel they're being rude I (the intellect) will deal with it, if you (my chimp) get involved, everyone will get hurt!" When you deal with your chimp it's important to tell it the TRUTH, don't try strong arm tactics as the Chimp is ten times stronger than you, it has to be to defend you." (The Chimp Paradox by Dr Stephen Peters)*

# Addendum 1 – Self Hypnosis MP3

Use this website url to access the audiofile for instructions of how to use a self hypnosis Track

http://emmajtriplett.com/wp-content/uploads/2017/08/Instructions-for-Using-Hypnosis-Tracks.m4a

Use this website url to access the self hypnosis MP3.
http://emmajtriplett.com/wp-content/uploads/2017/08/Old-Town-Hypnotherapy-Relxation-CD-1.mp3

# Addendum 2 – Mindfulness Meditation Practice

Follow the meditation for 20 minutes every morning

http://emmajtriplett.com/wp-content/uploads/2017/08/Guided-Mindful-Meditation.m4a

# Further Reading

http://emmajtriplett.com/goodbye-anxiety-adios-depression/

The Gold Standard six week intensive interactive video hypnotherapy and coaching course for people suffering from stress, anxiety and/or depression who are sick and tired of feeling sick and tired and have decided to take control of their life, learn how to resolve issues and move forwards.

Only for those people serious about getting their life back on track

# About the Author

### Emma Triplett
HPD, DPH, MNCH(Reg) AfSFH

Hypnotherapist, Psychologist & Life Coach

Emma is the Founder of Old Town Hypnotherapy Ltd, having opened the first branch in Swindon in 2011 after qualifying in Solution Focused Hypnotherapy at the prestigious Clifton Practice in Bristol.

Emma is no stranger to depression herself. In 2002 after a 15 year career in IT sales she crashed and burned out of the industry. The company doctor informed her she had depression and should be on antidepressants. At that time Emma knew nothing about depression and it wasn't until retraining as a solution focused hypnotherapist she understood the truth behind the perceived causes and is now determined to demystify depression, the misunderstanding and stigma around it, in particular the false belief that it is something you have to 'live with' for the rest of your life – it's simply not.

Emma's direct approach empowers people suffering from depression to take control of themselves and their lives and cure themselves of this horrible disease that affects not only them, but their families, friends and the world around them.

Emma has helped literally hundreds of people rid themselves of the life debilitating symptoms of anxiety and depression, opened 6 branches of Old Town Hypnotherapy in the UK and is now on a mission to empower others to make the internal changes necessary to rid themselves of these toxic diseases and live a happy, empowered and fulfilled life.

Emma is the owner and Director of Old Town Hypnotherapy Ltd and also runs her own Life Coaching business, www.emmajtriplett.com where she regularly holds Personal Development & Therapy Retreats on the Island of Gozo where she now lives.

*Emma J. Triplett*

## Contact Information

If you would like any further support, have specific questions, have difficulties accessing the meditation and hypnosis files or would like to get in touch for another reason, you can contact the author directly through her personal website http://emmajtriplett.com

Please always feel free to reach out for help

*Emma J. Triplett*

# Legal Notices

NOTICE: You DO NOT Have the Right to

Reprint or Resell this book

You Also MAY NOT Give Away, Sell or Share the Content Herein

All Rights Reserved

No part of this book may be reproduced or transmitted in any form whatsoever, electronic, or mechanical, including photocopying, recording, or by any informational storage or retrieval system without express written, dated and signed permission from the author.

Disclaimer and/or Legal Notices:

The information presented herein represents the views of the author as of the date of publication. Because of the rate with which conditions change, the author reserves the right to alter and update her opinion based on the new conditions. The book is for informational purposes only. While every attempt has been made to verify the information provided in this book, neither the author nor her affiliates/partners assume any responsibility for errors, inaccuracies or omissions. Any slights of people or organisations are unintentional.

The client stories are for example purposes only and no association is intended or should be made with any persons living or dead.

If advice concerning legal or related matters is needed, the services of a fully qualified professional should be sought.

# **Dedications**

A special thanks goes to David Newton HPD DHP SFBT(Hyp) SFBT Sup(Hyp) FAPHP MNCH MNCP SHS SQHP Sup Hyp, Hypnotherapist and Psychotherapist. It was David who introduced me to the concepts, theories and science presented in this book and taught me much of what I know. He changed my life and I owe him my deep gratitude and thanks.

Stepping Out Of The Cloud

Printed in Great Britain
by Amazon